COARSE FISHING

GARETH PURNELL

p

This is a Parragon Book

This edition published in 2005

Copyright © Parragon 1999

Parragon
Queen Street House
4 Queen Street
Bath BA1 1HE, UK

Designed, produced and packaged by
Stonecastle Graphics Ltd

Edited by Philip de Ste. Croix

ISBN 1-40544-711-7

Printed in Indonesia

Photographic credits
l = left, r = right, t = top, b = below

All pictures courtesy of **Gareth Purnell/EMAP
(Improve Your Coarse Fishing).**
Robin Griggs: artwork pages 21, 47, 51, 57.

CONTENTS

COARSE FISHING

IZAAK WALTON (1593-1683), regarded by many as the father of freshwater fishing, once likened angling to poetry. Perhaps he was referring to its qualities of relaxation, or of inspiration, or of its ability to inspire passion and obsession. Yet in the same book, *The Compleat Angler*, he observed that angling is like mathematics, in that it can never be fully learned. Both analogies are as true today as when he penned them long ago in the seventeenth century.

Despite massive advances in fishing tackle technology, angling still combines that infuriating blend of poetry and mathematics. One day pure joy, the next pure frustration! You will dream of those days when it all goes right. Those days when the rod tip pulls around at will, or the float dives under, and you connect with one fish after another, after another. But to appreciate such dream days, and you *will* have them, you also need to experience those sessions when there appear to be no fish within a mile of your bait. When the keepnet stays dry, the water freezes in the rod rings and the only bite you get is frostbite.

It is my belief that angling is either in your blood, or it isn't. Only those first few sessions will tell you whether you think it is worth enduring the bad times to appreciate the good. But if you have it, don't fight it! You have been blessed. You will have joined the millions who enjoy what for me is the greatest sport in the world.

In this section I have attempted to give a twentieth-century taste of the sport that inspired Izaak Walton to write his famous words. I have highlighted the kind of tackle you will need, included an outline of baits and techniques, and spotlighted the species you are likely to catch.

But the truth is that angling is forever on the move and you never stop learning. New tackle, revolutionary rigs, secret flavourings are constantly being revealed in the many angling magazines that proliferate on the newsagents shelves.

Only you can make the choice of whether you want to enjoy angling purely for pleasure, taking in the tranquillity of the countryside; or as a match angler, trying your all to beat the man at the next peg; or as a specialist, targeting certain species in a bid to catch that giant.

Whatever kind of angler you are, enjoy it. I hope you have more days of poetry than mathematics. Tight lines!

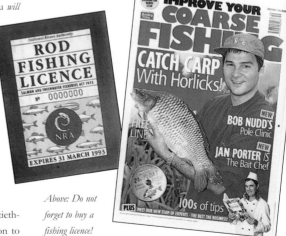

Above: Do not forget to buy a fishing licence!

Above right: Magazines help you to keep in touch with the latest fishing trends.

Right: Look forward to those dream days when everything goes according to plan.

WATERCRAFT

RIVERS

THE SECRETS OF SUCCESS

'There are three secrets to ensuring consistently good catches. Location, location and location.'

THERE ARE three secrets to ensuring consistently good catches and they are: location, location and location. In simple terms, if it is possible to identify where the fish like to congregate, even a novice angler will eventually be able to work out how to catch them. But even the best angler in the world cannot catch anything in a swim devoid of all things fishy.

Finding the so-called hotspots is no easy task, and one of the main reasons that experienced anglers catch so many more fish than beginners is that they have learnt something called watercraft, a far-reaching concept which could fill a whole book rather than just a few pages.

Watercraft is not only about targeting likely-looking swims along the river, although that is obviously the first step. Just as importantly, it encompasses decisions regarding in which part of the swim you should place the bait, and when to fish (and when not to fish), so that you are always maximizing your chances of success.

Choosing a Good Swim

What makes a good river swim? Well, it depends not only on what species you are targeting, and the time of year, but also on the venue itself. Broadly speaking, big fish do not like to fight against a strong current for too long, preferring to conserve their energy in the stretches that have a more evenly-flowing pace.

Above: Choose a well-oxygenated stretch of river to fish, such as this weirpool, when the weather is hot.

Right: Top English river angler Dave Harrell with a lovely catch of chub, taken on float tactics.

Left: River roach like to shoal up next to 'creases', where slow-flowing water meets faster-flowing water.
Below: Barbel will often feed heavily during winter flood conditions. Use a large, smelly bait to attract them in the coloured water.

TOP TIP

River swims which gradually become shallow downstream are often natural hotspots, as these are sloping areas where food builds up, so attracting fish.

Big fish will stay close to the bottom of the river, where the slower water they prefer meets the faster water bringing down morsels of food. From this position they can nip into the faster current to grab food as it passes. These are stretches through which the angler should run his bait, and luckily the presence of such areas of water are given away by what is called a crease – a disturbance on the water's surface indicating where the faster and slower bodies of water merge. Towards the inside curve of a bend in the river is a good place to look for creases.

In winter, when the weather gets really cold, fish tend to congregate in the deeper pools and holes in the river bed where they are protected from rapid changes in water temperature. In summer, fish may be more widely dispersed in a river because there is so much natural food about, and it is worth travelling to find it. Fish prefer well-oxygenated water during the summer months, so if your favourite river has a weirpool, this will be an especially good area to fish when the weather is hot.

The clarity of the water is important. If it is crystal clear, the fish will be able to see you just as well as you can see them. On such rivers you must adopt a careful, quiet, stalking approach, and look for pegs (convenient fishing areas) with far-bank cover, such as bushes and branches which drape into the water. Alternatively look for rafts of debris that have collected against a snag in the water, or evidence of under-cut banks. Fish as close to these features as you are able, or even under them if possible. You can be confident that this is where species like chub will spend the day, occasionally darting out to grab a meal.

The 'condition' of the river is vital too. You may find anglers thrashing a swim for days on end, catching little and moaning that 'the river isn't what it used to be'. Then, when the rain comes down and the river floods, the banks are deserted.

The expert fisherman will now be watching the river carefully. He knows that the floodwater will have put

'colour' (fine mud) into the river, giving fish the cover of which they were deprived in clear water and, consequently, more confidence to venture out in daylight. The fish will also expend more energy than usual as they combat the extra flow, and will soon need to feed heavily.

The experienced angler will be looking for just the right day, when the flow is subsiding and the colour is just starting to drop out of the water so he can see a short distance under the surface. Only then will he arrive on the river bank. He will use a large, smelly, highly visible bait like flavoured paste, bread, or a lobworm because he knows that the fish cannot see as far as usual and they will use a combination of sight and smell to locate a meal. And he will catch fish that other anglers can only dream of. Lesser anglers will call him lucky, but he is not. Far from it. He is using his years of experience to make sure he is fishing the right swim, in the right way, at the right time. That is watercraft.

STILLWATERS

TAKING TIME to choose a good swim on a stillwater is even more important than it is on rivers. That is because there is no flow to carry bait to fish and draw them into your peg. Instead, you must locate *them*.

It always pays to spend a few minutes looking at a venue after you arrive for a pleasure-fishing session to assess a number of important factors before you choose where to fish. The first thing to take into account is the wind direction. If there is a fairly strong prevailing wind, it will have blown items of food across the surface of the water, into one corner, attracting fish with it. Fishing into the wind may be uncomfortable, but it can often be very productive.

Natural Features

The next thing to look for is a natural feature, such as an island, a reed bed, or an area of lilies. Many commercial fisheries are completely flat and featureless below the water, with no sunken trees, snags or big drop-offs in depth. That is good for the angler. Fish are attracted to any features that will provide cover and safety, and on these venues the anglers can see all of them. If there is one over-riding rule, it is to fish as close to these features as you possibly can. You should look for a peg from which you can cast close to an island – within two or three feet (60-90cm) – or where you can drop your bait near to beds of reeds or lilies.

The biggest mistake that many anglers make on these commercial fisheries is to cast straight out in front of them into open water. Often the very best place to fish is about two feet (60cm) from the bank, right next to the reeds that are virtually under your feet. If the water is coloured, as it often is on these venues, fish will be there even if the water is only two feet (60cm) deep.

Gravel Pits

Gravel pit complexes present a completely different challenge. Gravel pits are like the surface on the moon under the water, with huge craters where the gravel has

Above: Do not be afraid to fish close in on commercial fisheries, particularly where there are natural features, such as reed beds.

Left: A superb gravel pit tench that fell for pre-baiting tactics is returned to the water.

A RULE TO REMEMBER

If there is one over-riding rule, it is to fish as close to natural features in the water as you possibly can.

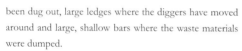

Left: On gravel pits you need to use a marker float and weight to plumb the bottom to locate underwater features.

Above: Carp will often be found close to reeds. They also cruise the margins taking food from the surface (below).

been dug out, large ledges where the diggers have moved around and large, shallow bars where the waste materials were dumped.

There is no particular pattern to their construction, and each pit will be different. A venue might plunge to a depth of 30 feet (9m) only 20 feet (6m) out, but in the middle it might be only four feet (1.2m) deep. This is a situation which requires you to spend time mapping out the pit to locate the features that will attract fish. But it is worth it, as gravel pits hold some huge specimen fish and many British records are achieved in such waters.

The first step to map out a gravel pit is a technique called 'leading', which is, essentially, plumbing the depth all over the venue. This involves using a 1-2oz (28-57g) lead tied to the end of your line with a 'marker float' above it (see picture). When you cast this rig out, the lead sinks to the bottom of the pit, and you retrieve line until the float is pulled down in the water until it hits the lead. Then you pay out line, a foot at a time (or in metric measurements) until the float appears at the surface. By counting how many feet you have released, you can calculate the depth of water at that point, and more importantly, you can measure any changes in the depth as you cast to different areas.

As you move from swim to swim, you can build up a picture (indeed many anglers actually draw a picture) of the sub-surface profile of the lake's bed. It is from this map that you can plan your attack.

In warmer months or during warm spells of weather in the winter, try fishing along the side of shallow bars, as

these are natural food larders and, therefore, excellent fish-holding areas. During cold weather, fish the deeper areas of the pit, where water temperatures will be warmest.

The time at which you fish is vital to success. On clear venues (and most gravel pits are clear) night fishing is the best time to catch fish, and this is particularly true on hard-fished venues. If you are unable to fish at night, try to fish on overcast, breezy days when the light intensity under the water will be low.

If you do catch a good fish, make a note of the time at which you caught it, as big fish in gravel pits generally have set feeding times which may only last for an hour each day.

Gravel pits are undoubtedly hard work compared with artificially-stocked commercial fisheries, but the rewards can be fantastic.

TACKLE

RODS

THE VAST majority of decent coarse fishing rods are now made from carbon-fibre as no other material can compete with its combination of strength, rigidity and lightness. But that is just the start of it, as you can buy rods from six to 20 feet (1.8 to 6m) long with as many different 'actions' as there are species of coarse fish.

I have used more rods than I care to remember, including fishing with an eight metre (26ft) telescopic 'Bolognese' rod in the world championships in Italy in 1996. While there is no doubt that having exactly the right tool for the job is useful, the best advice for the newcomer is to keep things simple.

Float Rods

Float rods tend to come in three sections of equal length and be 12 to 15 feet (3.7 to 4.6m) long and designed for use with lines or 2-4lb (0.9-1.8kg) breaking strain.

Rods for waggler fishing (see pages 18 and 42) tend to have a hollow tip section and plenty of 'give' below, which allows you to make long, sweeping strikes at a distance without the possible risk of snapping light hooklengths.

Above: Tackle shops are a good starting point to get advice about the type of rod that will suit your specific needs.

If you do a lot of stick float fishing (see pages 18 and 41) you will require a different action. With this technique you have to hit lighting-fast bites from wary fish, such as roach, and consequently stick float rods tend to be quite stiff up to the top two feet (60cm), allowing you to pick up line very quickly, but have a soft tip 'spliced' in to absorb the initial force of fast strikes into fish at short distances.

Unless you intend to concentrate on match or specialist fishing, it is advisable to buy one float rod, and spend as much as you can afford on it.

Overall, a hollow-tipped 13ft (4m) match rod with a nice snappy action, but a forgiving top third, will suit most pleasure fishing situations you are likely to come across.

Leger Rods

Leger rods are generally two-piece rods measuring between nine and 12 feet (2.7-3.7m) long and designed for use with lines of between 3-6lb (1.36-2.72kg) breaking strain. Most have either a screw thread or are hollow at the end, to accommodate the use of screw- or push-in swingtips or quivertips for bite indication. They usually have quite a forgiving (bendy) top half, but have plenty of power in the middle-to-lower section allowing you both to cast good distances and set hooks at that range.

Some of the better leger rods come with a selection of quivertips, and these are the best buy for the beginner. These tips will be of different strengths, measured by their test curve (the amount of dead weight it takes to pull the tip of the rod to an angle of 90 degrees to the handle) in ounces. A 2-3oz tip is stiff and designed to be used on fastish-flowing rivers, while 0.5-1oz tips are more suited to stillwater fishing.

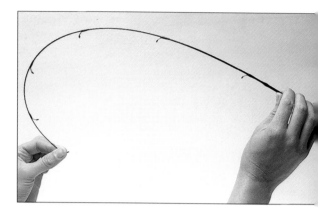

Above: Stick float rods have stiff bodies but feature very soft tips.

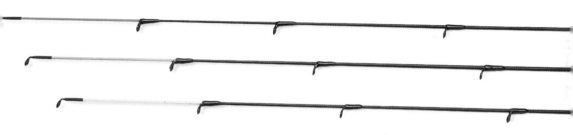

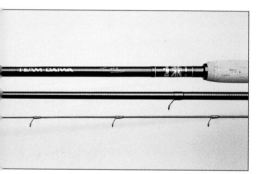

Above: Good leger rods are often supplied with a selection of different-strength quivertips.

Specialist rods

These two-piece rods of 11 to 13 feet (3.4-4m) length are measured by their test curve. They are designed for casting big baits and dealing with big fish, and tend to have much larger rings than leger and float rods. An ideal all-round choice for close-to-medium range fishing would be a 12ft (3.7m), 2lb (0.9kg) test curve rod with a medium to tip action, which means there is plenty of give in the top half of the rod to enjoy the fight of a big fish, but plenty of backbone in the lower half to allow you to cast big baits and bully fish away from snags.

Above left: Better rods usually have cork handles, plenty of rings and are thin where the carbon blank meets the handle.
Left: Many coarse fishing rods are manufactured with fixed fittings to hold the reel.

ROD TIP
Better rods tend to have plenty of rings, and to be quite thin where the carbon blank meets the cork handle.

REELS

REELS THAT are intended for coarse fishing can be divided into four main types, although most experienced anglers would undoubtedly recommend that beginners should start with the fixed-spool design.

Fixed-Spool Reels

These are by far the most commonly bought type of reel and without doubt they are the best choice for the beginner.

The line is carried on an open drum and is wound onto this static (fixed) spool by the bale arm, which revolves around it when the reel's handle is rotated. The spool moves in and out from the reel to ensure that the line is wound on evenly. To cast, the angler simply traps the line with his index finger, opens the bale arm, and flicks the rig out, letting go at the opportune moment.

Most good fixed-spool reels include some kind of adjustable drag system which provides resistance to a hooked fish, but allows line to be taken if the fish suddenly lunges. This slipping clutch is sometimes positioned at the front of the reel, but more commonly takes the form of a knob at the back.

The knob should be adjusted to a position whereby the reel will 'give' line although the bale arm is closed. This is your safety mechanism to avoid a hooked fish snapping the line and you possibly losing the fish of a lifetime as a consequence.

Most fixed spool reels have what is called a line clip on the side of the spool (see page 37). This is used when you need to cast really accurately, but only when you are not expecting to catch fish which are big enough to break the line. Simply cast to your chosen mark and wrap the line around the line clip. The next time you cast use just a little

Left and below: Fixed-spool reels are the easiest to use and the best choice for the novice angler.

TOP TIP

When loading a fixed-spool or a closed-face reel, you should ensure that the line comes right to the edge of the spool. This reduces friction against the edge of the spool when casting and makes for a smooth, accurate action.

Left: Centrepins are great to use, but tricky to cast with,

more force, and your cast will be stopped by the line clip and will be positioned exactly the same distance out from the bank as before.

Closed-Face Reels

With closed-face reels the spool is totally enclosed in a casing with only a small central hole through which the line emerges, making them invaluable for use in windy conditions. Instead of a bale arm, closed-face reels have a small pin around which line is gathered inside the housing. A gentle press on the front of the reel releases this spring-loaded pin, and by trapping the line with your finger, casting is achieved the same way as with a fixed-spool reel.

A single turn of the handle re-engages the pin, and then you can retrieve line. The spool itself is usually quite shallow and narrow, so these reels are best suited to light lines of no more than 2.5lb (1.1kg) breaking strain. They are the ideal reel for stick float fishing in windy weather, but are not suitable for catching big fish.

Centrepin Reels

Some anglers swear by centrepin reels. Certainly the line leaves the spool with a freedom unmatched by other types, but although they can be a joy to use, mastering these expensive reels is an artform and they are not a good choice for the beginner.

The best coarse fishing centrepins are 4.5 inches (11.4cm) in diameter with a body and drum machined from high quality aluminium stock, which revolves effortlessly around a central pin. On a good reel a gentle tap on the drum will send it spinning for over a minute. Some have solid-face drums, others have a series of holes drilled in the face to reduce the weight of the reel. Centrepins are tricky to use, but when the technique has been mastered, they are great reels for long trotting with a big 'top and bottom' float (see page 19).

Multiplier Reels

Some anglers consider multipliers to be the essential reel for big-pike fishing, and particularly so when using lures.

Multipliers operate on a revolving drum principle, with the line feeding from the front of the reel as the drum spins. They are great fun to use, but are prone to dreadful tangles in the hands of inexperienced anglers and are best left to the experts. However, many now have braking systems which cut down on over-runs (and tangles), although this feature tends to reduce casting distance.

Left: Closed face reels are ideal for fishing in windy conditions.

REELY GOOD

Multipliers have the simplest to use, and best, clutch system of any reel design, making them very popular with big-fish anglers.

Right: Multiplier reels are used by many top lure anglers.

LINES

FISHING LINE is fishing line, right? Wrong, I'm afraid. There are mainlines and hooklengths, including floating lines, sinking lines, braided lines and pre-stretched, hi-tech lines… Each of them has a specific use and it is important to have a basic understanding of each type, as selecting the wrong line can spell disaster.

Monofilament Lines

Ordinary monofilament lines are the first choice of most coarse anglers, and they come in many variations and boast various qualities. The vast majority of what anglers call 'mono' sold in the UK is made in Germany and Japan. Bayer Perlon, which floats, is a particularly popular choice for float fishing and Maxima, which sinks, is the top choice for legering.

Ordinary mono line stretches, is quite robust, and is the right choice for main line to put on the reel. There are many different colours from which to choose; from green to grey, brown to clear or even yellow.

For most float-fishing requirements 2-3lb (0.9-1.36kg) breaking strain would be a good choice, with 3-4lb (1.36-1.8kg) line a better strength for legering. Big carp and pike anglers should be using mainlines not lighter than 10lb (4.54kg).

Always use a hooklength, which must be less than the strength of the mainline, so that if you snag up you will only lose the hooklength.

As a general rule, the hooklength should have a breaking strain in the region of 10-20 per cent less than that of the mainline.

Pre-stretched Lines

Some lines are pre-stretched in order to reduce their diameter and so appear less obvious to the fish. They have a high breaking strain for their diameter compared with

Above: It really is a jungle out there for anyone new to the world of fishing line. There is a bewildering wealth of choice, but it is necessary to understand the specific qualities of each type of line before making your selection.

Right: Maxima is a popular choice of mainline, particularly for legering.

mono mainlines, but because they have had the stretch taken out of them during the manufacturing process, they are quite brittle and not suitable for use as mainlines.

They should be used only for hooklengths and for the mainline on pole rigs, where the pole's 'elastic' (a short length of elastic line) provides a cushion. Pro-Micron line is particularly popular, but because of the extra work that goes into making pre-stretched line, a spool is usually twice the price of ordinary mono.

Often you will read angling articles which refer to the diameter of the line in millimetres (e.g. 0.12mm), rather than to its strength. These are invariably pre-stretched lines, and although different makes have different breaking strains, a general guide to breaking strains is shown below.

DIAMETER OF LINE	BREAKING STRAIN
0.07mm	1.1lb
0.08mm	1.5lb
0.09mm	2lb
0.10mm	2.5lb
0.12mm	3lb
0.14mm	4lb
0.16mm	5lb

Braided Mainline

Braid is a weave of materials, rather like an ultra thin rope, and it can be used for either mainline or hooklengths. It is quite easy to tell which is which as mainline braids tend to be supplied in spools of at least 100m (330ft), whereas hooklength braids are usually in 10-20m (33-66ft) spools.

There has been quite a trend in favour of using braid as mainline in the last few years. The key feature of braid is that it has no stretch. This has proved a real boon for lure anglers, who say they can feel takes from pike, zander and perch that they would never have felt with mono on account of the latter's stretch.

Lure anglers need a sinking braid, such as Berkley Fireline or Gorilla Braid, although there are other brands which float and these are used by pike anglers who like to drift baits downwind using drifter floats. A sinking mainline would be a disaster with this technique.

Some carp and tench specialists also use the 'no stretch' factor to draw up a mental picture of what a venue is like underwater. They cast out a lead and bounce it along the bottom to 'feel' for gravel bars, which are a great fish

Left: Some manufacturers have begun to state the line's ideal use on the spool.

Above: Kryston make some great hooklength braids, which combine softness and fineness.

holding feature. It is amazing how you can feel every stone you bounce a lead over, even at 100m (330ft) when using braid.

Most rods are designed for use with monofilament lines, so it is essential to use a 'leader' of 8lb (3.6kg) mono for the last 25 feet (7.5m) or so of your rig.

Braided Hooklengths

Braided hooklengths are softer and more supple than braid used for mainline and they have a very small diameter for their strength compared to mono. It is this combination of softness and fineness, together with a high degree of resistance to abrasion compared to mono lines, that appeals to the specialists, who are often fishing for wary specimens in snaggy swims.

Big-fish anglers tend to use braided hooklengths of between six and 15 inches (15-38cm); many of the most popular brands are made by Kryston and Drennan.

A final word of warning though; braided hooklengths are much more expensive than their monofilament counterparts.

HOOKS AND KNOTS

Below: To make things simple, many manufacturers have started to indicate the hook's intended use on the packet. This is particularly helpful to the beginner who may find it difficult to select the ideal hook for each venue.

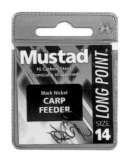

Left: There is a daunting range of hooks on the market, but it is a good idea for the new angler to keep things simple when making a choice.

THERE ARE hundreds of hook patterns on the market and it is hardly surprising that the beginner often makes an unsuitable choice. Luckily, manufacturers have begun to realise this and some are now stating clearly on the packet to which type of fishing each hook is suited.

In its simplest terms, you should be fishing small, fine wire hooks (e.g., size 18-22) with small baits (e.g., pinkie or maggot) for small fish (e.g., roach, dace and skimmer bream).

The bigger the fish you are after, the bigger and stronger the hook needs to be, as fine wire hooks will easily be bent straight or snapped by large, hard-fighting fish. You might, for instance, choose sizes 10-12 for chub fishing with a lump of breadflake, and size 4-8 for big carp fishing with a boilie as bait.

Strength Versus Presentation

The strength of the hook is vital, as it may be necessary to bully big fish away from snags in order to land them. Strength comes mainly from the 'gauge' of the wire used. The thicker it is, the stronger the hook is and those marked 'forged' are particularly power-packed and unlikely ever to bend, unless you hook 'Nessie'.

So why use fine wire hooks at all, you might ask? Why not use a nice, thick hook and be sure of landing every fish? Well, apart from the fact that a single maggot looks pretty silly on a size 8 hook, the answer is that basically fish are not as stupid as you might think.

Even small fish can be very wary of a big, thick piece of wire sticking out of a tasty-looking meal, and once they have been caught a few times, they begin to associate the hook's shape with danger. The smaller and finer the hook, the less likely they are to see it or feel it. This, of course, becomes a particular problem on hard-fished commercial fisheries which stock big fish, such as carp, that can

Above: Many anglers keep their hooks in well-labelled storage systems similar to this.

Left: It is a good idea for novice anglers to use pre-tied hooks to nylon, for general pleasure fishing.

Below: The Tucked Half Blood Knot is useful for attaching hooks, swivels or leads to the line.
The Four-turn Water Knot is a superb knot for attaching hooklengths to the mainline.

straighten out a fine wire hook in the blink of an eye. On these venues it might be necessary to fish size 20 hooks to get a bite, so it is essential to use a small hook made of strong wire. Thankfully manufacturers have responded to this need, and there are many such hooks on the market now, usually with 'Carp' or 'Power' marked on the packet somewhere.

There is another choice to make too. Hooks can be either 'eyed' and attached to the line with a knot through this eye, or 'spade end' which need to be attached with a whipping knot on the hook's shank.

The standard knot for attaching an eyed hook is a tucked half blood knot (see diagram) which is quite easy to master. Tying spade end hooks is much more difficult, but fortunately packets of pre-tied spade end hooks (called 'hooks to nylon') can be bought at any tackle shop. These should be attached to the mainline either 'loop to loop' or with a water knot (see diagram).

Barbs and Colours

Hooks can be barbed, barbless or have a microbarb. The barb helps hold a live bait like a maggot or worm on the hook, and it also can help to hold a hooked fish. However, as long as you keep a tight line between the rod and the

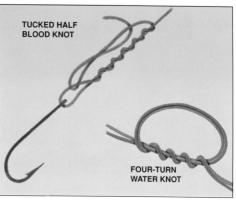

TUCKED HALF BLOOD KNOT

FOUR-TURN WATER KNOT

fish when playing it, barbless hooks are suitable. Many commercial fisheries insist on the use of barbless hooks to minimize damage to the fish. Microbarbed hooks have a tiny barb just below the point and are ideal for pole fishing.

You can buy hooks in many different colours – silver, bronze, gold, black, green and even red. However, it is far more important to choose the right size and pattern of hook than to worry about the choice of colour.

There are also many different shapes of hooks, with varying shank lengths and curves, resulting in an almost unbelievable choice. Experience is the best guide and all anglers eventually discover their own favourites.

Beginners are recommended to go for pre-tied spade ends for general pleasure fishing, such as the Drennan Team England Super Carbon Maggot range, or the Drennan Carbon Feeder range. For more specialist fishing, such as targeting barbel or chub, it is necessary to choose a stronger pattern, such as the Drennan Specimen, Carbon Specimen or the Drennan Superspecialist.

THE AUTHOR'S FAVOURITE HOOKS
POLE FISHING: Kamasan B511, Drennan Ultra Fine Pole.
WAGGLER FISHING: Tubertini Series 2, Maver Katana C032.
FEEDER FISHING: Mustad 90340, Drennan Carbon Chub.
SPECIMEN FISHING: Drennan Carbon Specimen, Drennan Specimen, Drennan Superspecialist.

FLOATS

ANYONE NEW to angling is likely to be completely baffled by the selection of floats available in tackle shops these days. There are wagglers, stick floats, loafers, pencils, dibbers, balsas, toppers, Avons and sliders. There are floats with wire stems and cane bristles, cane stems and nylon bristles, carbon stems and cane bristles. There are floats which are designed to carry just two or three tiny shot, and there are floats which need 0.35oz (10g) of weight or more to set correctly.

Even if you ask for a waggler in your local tackle shop, it is not a simple request. You might be asked if you would like an insert or a straight waggler, a bodied or loaded waggler, a crystal or a peacock!

All of these strangely named floats are designed for specific situations and different types of fishing. The question is, where do you start to negotiate your way through the float fishing maze? For a start, there is no way that the beginner can expect to understand the uses of all the floats on the market. Indeed you could fish for a lifetime and never need to use 50 percent of them. A better idea is to try and understand a basic range of floats and the theory behind them.

Wagglers

Wagglers are floats which are attached to the line through a ring at the bottom end. The float is locked in place with a split shot on either side, and then more pieces of shot are added until only about a half of an inch (1.25cm) of the bright tip is showing above the surface film. They are used on both still and flowing water, with different types functioning best in different depths. As a basic rule, the

Right: Wagglers are attached to the mainline at the bottom end only, locked in place with split shot. They can be used on rivers and stillwaters. Below: There is an amazing array of floats available in tackle shops. Most anglers build up a collection of various types and styles of floats for using at different venues and when fishing for specific species of fish.

Left: Stick floats are designed for use on running waters and are attached to the line with silicone rubbers.

Right: Pole floats are attached with the line running first through a small eye at the top of the stem and then through two silicone rubbers on the stem.

further it is necessary to cast and the deeper the water, the heavier the waggler that is required.

Loaded wagglers are also available. These carry weight already within the base of the float, so that less shot is needed to cock them in the water.

Stick Floats

Stick floats are for use in running water. They are attached to the line by hollow rings of soft silicone in what is termed 'top and bottom' fashion (see page 41). That simply means that the line from the rod is fastened to the top of the float, rather than to the bottom, as in the case of wagglers. This arrangement allows the angler a great deal of control over the behaviour of the float as it runs downstream, with the possibility of slowing the float down or even holding it still against the water's flow. Using this method it is possible to 'tease' the bait and alter its presentation, thus tempting bites from shy or wary fish.

Stick floats may be manufactured from cane (for close-in work) or lignum (for casting greater distances) or be wire stemmed (for turbulent water).

Pole Floats

It is impossible to cover the entire range of available pole floats in a short space, such is the massive range available

to the angler. However, the majority are attached to the line by two small silicone bands on the stem below the body, with the line passing through an eye in the top half of the float. If the float's shape is 'body up' (with the bulbous body of the float near the top of the stem), it is designed for use in running water so that it can be held back in a flow. If it is 'body down', it is a stillwater float.

Generally speaking, wire and carbon stems are used for fishing on the bottom and offer good stability in choppy water, while cane-stemmed floats are used for fishing on the drop or in the upper layers of the water.

Pike Floats

Pike floats are much bigger than wagglers, pole floats or stick floats, basically because they are designed to have sufficient buoyancy to suspend a live or dead fish underneath without submerging.

Many pike floats have a hollow centre through which the line is threaded. This allows them to slide up the line until they meet a small stop knot, set to match a pre-determined depth of water.

Right: Pike floats must be big enough to suspend a live, or dead, fish without sinking.

BITE INDICATION

A SSUMING THAT you are set up with all the necessary tackle, the next step is to select a method of bite indication that suits your requirements. It is easy when you are float fishing. You counterbalance the float with shot so that only half an inch (1.25cm) of the float is showing above the water, and if the float goes under, you have got a bite. This can even work at night, thanks to 'starlites' and 'isotopes' which glow in the dark and which you can see up to about 33ft (10m) from the water's edge.

If you are legering, however, things are different, and there are several forms of bite indication to choose from, depending on the species for which you are fishing.

Quivertips

A stiff but slightly flexible tip is fitted into the end of the rod. You cast out your leger or feeder, place the rod in the rod rests, and tighten up the line until there is a small bend in the quivertip. A bite is registered when the tip moves round or drops back.

There are three sorts of quivertip. The 'push-in' tip, which simply pushes into a hollow at the end of your leger rod; the 'screw-in' tip, for attaching to rods with a thread fitting at the end; and the 'push-over' tip, in which the tip is attached to the rod by pushing it over the end of the rod, rather than into a hollow. I prefer push-in tips, and several leger or feeder rods on the market are manufactured with three different strengths of tip to suit different conditions.

The relative strength of quivertips are measured by test curve in ounces. A 0.5oz tip is ideal for stillwaters on calm days, a 1oz tip is right for stillwaters on windy days and slow-flowing rivers, a 2oz tip is correct for a medium-paced river, and so on.

Swingtips

Swingtips attach in a similar manner to quivertips but instead of following the line of the rod, they hang down because of a flexible piece of silicone close to the attachment. The angler casts in, puts the rod in the rod rests and sets the tip so that it hangs down vertically at a 90-degree angle from the end of the rod. A bite is registered when the tip moves towards the rig or drops back.

Swingtips offer superbly sensitive bite indication on stillwaters because there is almost no tension for the fish to detect, and they are often used by bream and roach

Above: Quivertips are one of the most popular forms of bite indicator.
Right: The swingtip offers superbly sensitive bite indication on stillwaters.

anglers. However, they are not suitable for flowing water, because the flow straightens out the tip and renders bite detection impossible.

Bite Alarms

Bite alarms offer an audible indication of a bite, allowing the angler freedom to take his eyes off the indicator, and they are generally used in the pursuit of big fish by specialists who may be fishing for just one specimen fish per session.

Bite alarms are a real boon for night fishing for obvious reasons. The angler casts out and places the rod in the rests, pointing the rod tip towards the rig. The bite alarm is used as the front rod rest – the mainline is positioned in a groove in the alarm where it sits over a tiny roller. When a fish picks up the bait and takes line, the roller moves so setting

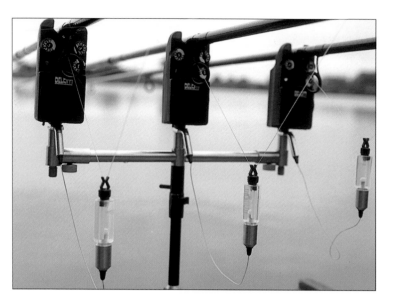

Left: Bite alarms are used as front rod rests and offer an audible, as well as visual, bite indicaton. Here they are used in addition to bobbins which simply clip onto the line and register any movement.

Below: A monkey climber works on the same principle as a bobbin, but slides up and down a fixed, vertical pin as the line is taken by a fish

off the alarm signal. In addition an LED light comes on so that the night angler can see which rod has a 'run'. Bite alarms are usually also used in conjunction with one of the indicators described below as a visual bite indicator.

Bobbins and Monkey Climbers

These may be any form of simple attachment which hangs on the line between the reel and the rod's first ring and which moves up or down to signal a bite. The angler casts in and puts the rod in the rests, pointing at the rig. He then tightens up the slack line, attaches the bobbin and pays line off the reel until the bobbin hangs down several inches. When a fish takes the bait, the bobbin moves up or drops, depending on which way the fish is running.

The monkey climber is very similar to a bobbin, but it incorporates a steel pin which sticks into the ground and makes the set-up stable in a wind. The bobbin slides up and down the pin when a fish takes the bait. Most good bobbins have a fitting so that you can attach isotopes for night fishing. They are best used with running leger rigs rather than 'bolt rigs' (see page 51).

Swingers

Swingers are more advanced indicators designed specifically for carp fishing. They attach to the front bankstick, usually underneath the bite alarm. An arm hangs down with a clip fitting at the end, to which an isotope can be added and into which the mainline clips. A weight on the swinging arm can be adjusted to suit wind

conditions. The line is released from the clip when the angler strikes. Swingers are usually used in conjunction with a bolt rig.

Springers

These are another advanced carp fishing indicator which hold the line under tension and actually spring off the line when a fish takes the bait, helping to set the hook. They should be positioned in a similar manner to swingers and, again, they are usually used with a bolt rig set-up.

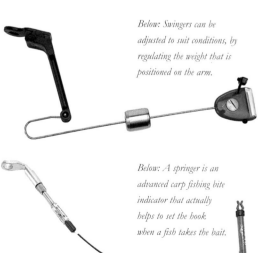

Below: Swingers can be adjusted to suit conditions, by regulating the weight that is positioned on the arm.

Below: A springer is an advanced carp fishing bite indicator that actually helps to set the hook when a fish takes the bait.

ACCESSORIES

Above: Plastic disgorgers are a good choice; they float and don't rust.

A S YOU read through this section you will see that I have highlighted certain accessories that you need for specific types of fishing. However, there are other items which every angler needs to ensure a comfortable and successful day's fishing.

Here I will cover the bare essentials, but you only have to walk around a tackle shop to see just how many accessories are marketed for anglers. Do not think you have to go out and buy the lot before you start fishing. It is simply a case of building up your tackle collection as your fishing progresses, to suit the type of fish you are targeting.

Disgorgers

Disgorgers are a vital piece of kit for ensuring that hooks can be quickly and safely removed from a fish. You will need a micro-disgorger for hook sizes of 22 and smaller, and a normal-sized disgorger for hooks between size 14 and 20. For larger hooks it is much better to use a pair of forceps if a fish is hooked awkwardly. The best disgorgers are made from plastic, because if you drop them in the water they will float. Middy make one with a micro-disgorger at one end and a normal one at the other.

Landing Nets

There are many different sorts of landing nets available. For river fishing you will need one with quite a wide mesh so that the flow of the water passes through it easily and does not drag the net out of your hands when you attempt to land a fish. Fine-meshed landing nets are designed for stillwaters and you should select one to suit the type of fish you are going to catch. Very shallow 'pan' nets are really for canal fishing. If you are likely to catch bigger fish, such as carp and tench, buy deeper one. Triangular, oval and round nets are all available and really the shape you choose is a matter of personal preference. Specimen nets are huge and are for the big carp, pike or catfish angler.

Keepnets

As with landing nets, there are all manner of keepnets on the market. The best choice for the beginner is to select one of around 10ft (3m) in length with a fine mesh. Choose a keepnet which has a device which allows it to be locked at various angles. Good manufacturers include Keenets, Drennan International and Waterline.

Bank Sticks

Every angler needs a selection bank sticks into which he can screw rod-rest heads, bait trays, keepnets and the like. The best bank sticks are extendible and have a tough, solid point which pushes easily into the ground. The best I have seen are the Dinsmores Arrow Points. Do not be tempted to use a bank stick as a handle for your landing net; buy a purpose-designed landing-net handle instead.

Catapults

If you are fishing more than about 15 feet (4.6m) from the bank you will need a catapult to feed the swim. You can buy pole catapults for feeding accurately up to about 50ft (16m), match catapults for waggler fishing up to about 80ft (25m), and groundbait catapults for firing balls of groundbait up to 100ft (30m). I use catapults made by Drennan for loosefeed, and by Seymo for groundbait.

Seat Boxes

You are going to need something to sit on while you wait for a bite, and for beginners you cannot beat the plastic seat boxes made by Shakespeare and Daiwa. They have comfortable carrying straps, plenty of room for your tackle inside and you can also buy trays that fit to the side of them into which to put all your bits and pieces of tackle. You can also get your local tackle dealer to fit

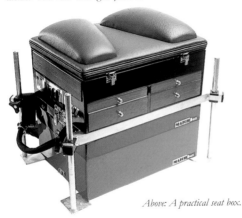

Above: A practical seat box.

Split shot.

Octoplus levelling legs which can be a real boon on sloping banks. If you make progress in your angling, you might want to buy a more expensive 'continental' box. These have integral levelling legs and integral side and front trays for your bits and pieces, and cushioned seats. Many can have wheels fitted to ease those long walks along the bankside. Good makes include Boss and Brilo.

Split Shot and Olivettes

Split shot are used to weight your float down so that only a little piece of the tip is showing above the water. Sizes are (from largest to smallest): SSG, SG, AAA, AA, BB, 1, 4, 6, 8, 9, 10, 11, 12, 13, 14. The larger sizes are placed around the base of the float to make up about four-fifths of the total weight required, with smaller shot, such as 8s, strung out beneath. For many pole-fishing situations, most of the weight is placed in a bulk about two-thirds of the way down the line with a couple of tiny shot strung out beneath. Instead of using shot for the bulk, you can buy olivettes which are measured in grammes. In their larger sizes, split shot are also used for link legering (see page 49).

Rod Rests

These are another essential item of equipment for all types of angling. For legering, the best are those with several rod grooves, as they allow for careful setting of the quivertip. For float fishing, those with a soft band on which to place your rod are the choice as these help to protect your rod.

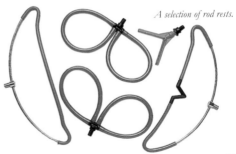

A selection of rod rests.

BAITS

NATURAL BAITS

Y OU CAN talk all you like about secret rigs, fancy tackle and deadly flavourings, but the undeniable truth is that if the fish that you are pursuing does not like the bait you are presenting, you will not catch it.

Here follows a brief guide to some of the main baits used by anglers, together with advice on how to present them on the hook, and when to use them. But the best advice is to keep experimenting with a variety of baits, and methods of presentation, until you have discovered the correct combination for any particular day.

Strange though it may seem, fish feed differently from one day to another and although a large lump of paste might catch your chub on Saturday, you might have to use a single maggot on Sunday to achieve success.

Above: Maggots, pinkies, squatts and casters. Some of the most popular natural baits. Right: The largest one is a maggot, the middle one is a squatt and the top one is a pinkie.

Maggots

Maggots are the larvae of the bluebottle, and they are the standard method of attack for most pleasure anglers. Most tackle shops sell maggots, and they can be bought in a variety of colours, including white, red and bronze, the latter being particularly popular for river fishing. Maggots are usually sold in pint, or half pint, measures.

When fresh, maggots have a large black spot near their pointed end. They should be hooked through the blunt head end, using a hook sized between 16 and 20.

Pinkies

Pinkies are the larvae of the greenbottle, and are about half the size of a maggot. They are a good alternative bait to maggots, when the fish you are catching are small, or particularly shy-biting as they may be during the winter months. Not surprisingly, they are usually pink in colour, but they are also available in white, red, bronze and fluoro pink.

Pinkies sink more slowly in water than maggots, and so are not really suitable for loosefeeding in deep water. They should be hooked in the same manner as for maggots. Use hook sizes 18-22.

Left: This is the correct way to present a caster, with the hook buried inside the shell.

Right: Lobworms are an excellent natural bait for many species of fish, including perch, carp and chub.

Squatts

These are the larvae of the housefly, and are much smaller than pinkies. They are usually sold in damp red sand and can be bought coloured either white or red at most tackle shops. They should be used as a hookbait as a last resort, or if the fish you are catching are particularly small, as may be found in some canals.

Squatts are not very lively creatures, which makes them an excellent bait for packing into groundbait for 'balling in', or fishing through an open-ended groundbait swimfeeder. They are an excellent holding bait for bream. Use hook sizes 20-26 if you decide to use them as bait.

Casters

Casters are the chrysalis stage of maggots, before they emerge as flies. When maggots first metamorphose into casters, their shells are pale and they will readily sink in water. However, they turn dark brown when left in the open air and rapidly become 'floaters'. Generally speaking, anglers want casters to sink. They can be stopped from turning into floating casters by keeping them immersed in water, or sealed in an air-tight bag, which is how they are sold in tackle shops.

Casters are a good bait for attracting the quality fish in the swim, and they are particularly liked by roach. They should be hooked by threading the caster around the hook's bend, so burying the whole hook inside the shell. Use hooks sized 16-18.

Lobworms

Lobworms are an excellent bait for targeting big fish from rivers in flood conditions, or for catching big perch. They are best kept in either the soil you dug them from, or better still, in grass cuttings, which has the benefit of toughening the worm's skin. Lobworms can be collected from most lawns at night, after it has rained, when they come to the surface.

THE GREAT ESCAPE

Maggots and pinkies are great escapers when wet, so if it starts raining, make sure they are secured in a tightly-covered container.

Hook lobworms through the head using a hook sized between 8 and 12.

Dendrobaenas

These are middle-sized worms. They are an excellent feeder bait when chopped up and tipped into the water from a pole cup or bait dropper, or when added to groundbait for bream fishing. As a hookbait it is best to use a piece of a dendra, hooked at the cut end. They can be bought from most tackle shops, or even by mail order. Use hook sizes 10-16.

Redworm

Quite easy to collect from compost heaps, the redworm is a first-class bream bait, particularly when 'tipped' with a maggot or caster.

Triple world champion Bob Nudd likes to present a redworm by cutting it in half and hooking both pieces at the cut ends. He believes that the fish are attracted to the cut (hook) end which is letting out all the lovely juices. Use hook sizes 14-18.

Right: Redworms appear to be an irresistible bait for bream, and can be collected easily from compost heaps.

BREAD AND PARTICLE BAITS

Breadflake

Bread is a superb all-round bait which will take fish of all species and sizes when used in its many forms. The fluffy white flake from an uncut loaf is particularly attractive to cyprinids, and its advantages to the angler include the fact that it is highly visible, soft, buoyant and easy to flavour. It is also easy to present on the hook. Just take a piece of breadflake, fold it around the shank of the hook and pinch it, leaving the point showing.

For fishing over weeds, or on the surface, use a piece of flake with the crust attached. Use hook sizes 10-14

Bread Punch

This is a very good bait for catching roach in clear water, when used in conjunction with liquidized bread feed, which you can either make yourself or buy as 'punch crumb' in tackle shops.

Bread punches are usually available in sets, with a variety of different-sized heads that will press out neat pellets from bread, to suit the type of fish you are after. Fresh, sliced white bread will achieve the best results.

Using a hook of between 14 and 22 in size, push the point through the slot at the side of the bread punch and turn the hook to fasten it into the bread pellet.

Hemp

Hempseed does not look very impressive, but it is probably the best holding bait for fish in both still and

Above: Bread punch is great for catching roach in clear water.

running water. A 'maggot and hemp' attack is a standard approach for many match, and pleasure, anglers.

You can buy hemp in tackle shops, already cooked, or prepare your own, which is actually very simple. to do. Simmer the hempseed until the shells start to split and the white kernel appears. It is this kernel that the fish love. Fortunately, hemp freezes well so you can prepare enough for several sessions at one time.

Hemp can be fished on the hook, and although this is quite difficult and requires precise presentation, it can be deadly for big roach. In fact, on some hard-fished venues roach will almost never take a maggot but can be caught quite easily on what anglers call 'the magic seed'. Use seeds which have only just split and use the shell itself to help clamp the bait to the hook. Use hooks sized 16-20.

Tares

These are a superb summer bait on venues with plenty of roach of 4oz (113g) or bigger. They are usually fished in conjunction with hemp loosefeed but because of their larger size, tares tend to attract the bigger fish.

Tares are like hard, black peas when bought from the tackle shop, and are quite easy to prepare simply by boiling in water for about 40 minutes until they have become soft. Adding a teaspoonful of bicarbonate of soda when the

> **GETTING THE POINT**
> When fishing with bread paste or flake, always ensure that the point of the hook is showing, and is not masked by the bait.

Above: Breadflake is a very useful all-round bait for many species.

tares are nearly cooked turns them an attractive purplish-black colour. They are hooked simply by pushing the point in and out of the skin, leaving plenty of the hook showing. As with hemp, it can take a couple of hours of regular feeding for the bait to start working, but if you do get the roach feeding on either, you could be in for the catch of a lifetime. Use hooks sized 16-18.

Sweetcorn

Sweetcorn is an ideal bait because it is cheap and can be used straight from the tin. It is an excellent summer bait for big fish, in particular carp, barbel and tench. Quite recently, ready-flavoured and coloured sweetcorn has become available, so you can now use anything from red, strawberry-flavoured corn, to orange Tutti Frutti corn. A company called Pescaviva even produce these permutations in liquidized form as well. Golden corn is particularly useful because it is highly visible in clear water.

There are various ways to present corn on a hook, but whichever you choose, try to cover as much of the hook's shank as possible, leaving the point free. Use one piece of sweetcorn on a size 16 hook, two pieces on a size 12, and so on as hook sizes increase.

Right: Hempseed is a useful holding bait for many species of fish.

Below: Sweetcorn is a cheap, convenient bait for big fish.

MAN-MADE BAITS

ONE OF the greatest thrills in angling is to catch a big fish on a bait that you have concocted yourself, especially if you have tried a 'secret' bait, ingredient or flavour which nobody else knows about.

To cater for the need to experiment, there are now bait companies marketing a wide variety of colours, additives and flavours for you to add to your pastes, boilies and groundbait. In addition, your local supermarket is full of potential baits that you can use straight from the tin or packet.

Here is a brief description of the man-made baits which have accounted for the majority of big fish in recent seasons.

Pastes

As well as being good fun to make, pastes are an excellent bait for chub, carp, barbel and tench. The basis of paste is a fluffy white loaf of bread – at least four or five days old – with the crust cut off. Soak the bread in water until it is soggy, then squeeze out as much water as you can and wrap the mass in an old tea cloth or, better still, a piece of muslin. Wring this out as firmly as possible and you will be left with a doughy mass. At this point you can add all manner of flavours, colours, cheeses and the like as you knead the bread into a paste. 'The smellier the better' is my motto when it comes to pastes, and I particularly like adding Stilton cheese for chub fishing in the winter.

Above: You can make your own paste, or buy it ready-made and flavoured from a wide selection available at tackle shops.

Above: Boilies and meat baits should be presented on a hair rig.

Paste should be firm enough to stay on the hook during casting, but soft enough to come off the hook as you strike at a bite. If your paste is too soft, you can firm up the mixture by adding a small amount of flour.

Several companies market mixes which just need the addition of water, and trout pellet paste is particularly effective for catching carp. All pastes should be hooked so that the paste covers the whole of the hook shank and bend, but with the tip of the point showing. Paste can be used with hooks of sizes ranging from 6 to 14.

Boilies

Boilies are frequently misunderstood by non-carp anglers. Put simply, boilies are essentially small balls of paste, which have had egg added and which are then boiled so as to create hard outer shells which small fish cannot nibble away at.

These days you can buy base mixes from tackle shops, which contain all sorts of lovely proteins, fats and vitamins, and which mix easily into a paste. To turn the paste into boilies, add eggs, flavours and colours to the mixture, and roll it into small balls, and then boil them in water for about 90 seconds. Leave them to dry, and after a few hours the skin will have hardened enough to use. Any boilies not required for an immediate fishing session can be stored in the freezer.

Boilies are fun to make and it is not difficult to produce good results, but there are several companies manufacturing ready-made boilies which are ideal for beginners, or for those anglers with limited time. Manufactured boilies are sized in millimetres, by diameter, and should be fished on a 'hair rig' using hooks between 4 and 10 in size. Boilies will take carp, tench, chub and barbel.

Cheese

Cheese works well when incorporated into pastes but can also be fished straight from the packet. The rubbery cheeses like Edam and Gouda are best as they stay on the hook firmly and withstand constant pecking from small fish. Smelly cheeses like Danish Blue are good on rivers in flow conditions. Cheese is an excellent chub bait and should be fished in cubes with the hook point sticking out. Use hooks sized 6-12.

Processed meat

Processed meats are particularly attractive to chub, barbel and carp. Luncheon meat is probably the most popular meat bait and is usually fished in cubes on a hair rig, or directly on the hook. Other commonly used meat baits include peperami, cat food and hotdog sausages. Use hooks sized 6-14.

Dog biscuits

Floating dog biscuits, in particular Chum Mixer, are a super summer carp bait, and they will also tempt other species including chub. Out of the box they are hard, and as a result quite tricky to hook. The best method is to cut a groove in one side of the biscuit and glue the back of the shank of a large hook into the groove using superglue. They are quite easy to flavour and colour, and should be fished in conjunction with a controller float. Use hooks sized 10-12.

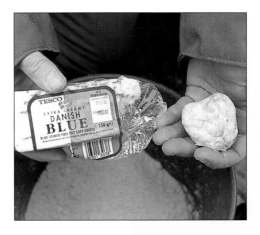

Above: Smelly cheeses, such as Stilton and Danish Blue, will attract fish when fishing rivers that are in flood.

Below: Luncheon meat is a classic bait for carp, barbel and chub. It is best cut into cubes and fished on a hair rig.

FISHY SPICE

Luncheon meat can be flavoured by frying it for about a minute in oil mixed with your chosen flavours. Spicy flavours are best in winter, and sweet flavours in summer.

Left: Peperami and other processed meats make excellent baits for big fish.

GROUNDBAIT

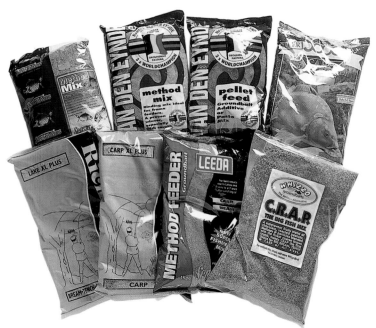

TOP TIP

Do not use live
maggots in balls of
groundbait for
catapulting into the
water. They move
about too much and
will break up the balls
in mid-flight.

*Left: There is plenty of choice
when it comes to selecting
groundbait. Fortunately,
many manufacturers state on
the packaging the intended use
for each of their different
types of groundbait.*

GROUNDBAIT IS used to attract fish into the swim and to keep them in a tight area on, or close to, the bottom. It can be fed into the water in balls, thrown in by hand at distances of up to about 45 feet (14m), or through a special groundbait catapult with a range of approximately 100 feet (30m). Alternatively, an open-ended feeder attached to the line will carry the groundbait as far as you can cast.

In its simplest form, groundbait is dried and crushed bread. Anglers call this 'crumb' and, when laced with squatts, this is the best mix for bream fishing.

In recent years, so-called Continental groundbaits containing all sorts of unusual ingredients in addition to bread have begun to occupy an increasing amount of space on the shelves of tackle shops. Several brands are designed specifically for enticing one particular kind of fish and, luckily for the beginner, this is usually stated on the packaging. For instance, French groundbait manufacturers, Sensas, market a range of separate groundbaits under the names Roach, Tench, Bream and Carp.

Manufacturers tend to keep the actual contents of their mixes secret to prevent them being copied. You

cannot blame them; there are not too many other businesses where the customer pays good money for a product which he immediately throws away!

It's in the Mix

In addition to choosing mixes to suit individual species, you should also consider the venue you will be fishing. For a deep, fast-flowing river, you will need a groundbait that binds together strongly so it will drop down to the bottom without breaking up. The flow of water will then help to break down the balls of groundbait. On a shallow lake, however, a mixture of this type would be useless, as the ball would just sit on the bottom without breaking up. A much lighter mix which starts disintegrating as it hits the water is needed.

Many companies actually take the trouble of stating for which kind of venues and fishing methods each of their mixes is best suited, including the ideal depth of water.

Breaking Up

You can get any mix to behave differently just by varying the amount of water you add. The drier the mix, the quicker it will break up on contact with water.

Generally speaking, it is necessary to create a mix which will hold together as it enters the water, but will break up close to the bottom. If you can produce a fine groundbait that will do this, it will create an attractive cloud close to the bottom, and this can prove deadly to fish on clear, hard-fished stillwaters.

You can also change the performance of groundbait by adding PV1 Colant – a powerful powder binder – which is extremely effective. PV1 powder should be added to the dry ingredients of the groundbait before mixing with water; the more you use, the harder the balls will be.

Flavours and additives

In tandem with the boom in groundbait has come a veritable cornucopia of flavours and additives. These are available in liquid, or powder, form and most state on the packaging which species they are designed to lure. Liquid flavours should be added to the water that you use to mix with the groundbait, whereas powders are mixed with the dry groundbait before adding water. Much research has gone into additives and some top specialist and match anglers are enthusiastic fans. It is generally believed that sweet flavours are best in the summer, and spicy flavours in winter.

Below: To mix groundbait, pour the dry ingredients into a bowl and stir them well. Then add water, a little at a time, mixing constantly until the groundbait is damp enough to hold together when squeezed, but will still break up quite easily. Now add any loosefeed to the mixture. Mould the groundbait into small balls.

ARTIFICIAL LURES

L URES ARE designed to mimic the fish which predators eat naturally and since fish like pike, bass, perch, chub and zander will take virtually anything at times, lures come in a bewildering array of colours, shapes and sizes. They have great names too, like the Crazy Crawler and the Creek Chub Pike. There is plenty of fun to be had building a collection of lures to suit differing venues and conditions.

For most freshwater fishing you choose from a variety of plugs and spinners. Plugs wobble with an upright motion though the water, whereas spinners have a blade that rotates around an axis creating a spinning action, as the name suggests.

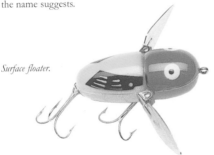

Surface floater.

Most plugs are made from a single piece of painted wood, plastic or metal and can basically be divided into three categories – surface plugs (also known as poppers), floating divers and sinking divers.

Plugs up to three inches (7.6cm) in length are ideal for catching perch and chub, but for pike fishing you can use plugs up to 12 inches (30.5cm) long.

Surface Plugs

Surface plugs are the most fun to use, as you can see the action of the lure as it pops, weaves, rattles and gurgles its way along the surface. Takes from pike in particular can be unforgettable as the predator surges from the deeper water to take the lure on the surface with a spectacular splash. Many plugs look nothing like any natural food that a predator would normally take, but the vibrations transmitted across the surface of the water as the plug is retrieved seem to trigger their natural aggression. The fish probably thinks it is taking a frog, water rat or vole that is swimming on the surface.

Surface plugs are most successful when fished close to lily beds, reed lines and over weed beds in no more than

Floating diver.

Jerkbait.

TOP TIP

Use a wire spinning trace at all times when lure fishing. All predators have sharp teeth and most of them can bite through ordinary mono line.

ten feet (3m) of clear water. Famous surface plugs include the Heddon Crazy Crawler, the Jitter Bug and the Heddon Zara Mouse.

Floating Divers

Known as crank baits in America, these are the most versatile of all artificial lures as they can be fished along the surface on a slow retrieve or made to dive beneath the surface by retrieving the line much faster (called 'cranking'). They have a vane at the front and this determines the plug's action. Those with a large, low-angled vane will dive deeply when cranked in, whereas those with smaller, sharply-angled vanes work at a much shallower depth. Good floating divers to have in your collection include the Shakespeare Big S, the Rapala Shad Rap, the Abu Hi-lo, the Booker Tail Crankbait and the Rapala Fat Rap Deep Runner.

Jerkbaits

These are large single and jointed lures designed to catch big predators. Much of the action is imparted through the skill of the angler who must use powerful tackle to cast these heavy lures and get them working. They are available in floating, sinking or shallow diving forms, but they are not lures for the beginner.

Sinking Divers

These sink when cast into the water and allow you to explore different depths using the same lure, depending on the point at which you start the retrieve and the speed at which you retrieve. One of the classics is the Creek Chub Pike (pictured right), the lure which captured the current British pike record of 46lb 13oz (21.23kg). This pattern comes in single and jointed versions and can be either wobbled speedily just under the surface, or allowed to sink deeper and worked slowly along the bottom.

Spinners

Spinners tempt fish through their combination of visual attraction and the vibrations that are transmitted into the water as a metal blade revolves around a fixed stem. The most famous spinners are made by Mepps, and in the smaller sizes (00 to 1) these are fabulous perch and chub lures. Similar spinners are made by Rublex, Landa and Abu.

Spinnerbaits

These crazy-looking lures are designed to catch American bass, but they have also been found to be very successful in attracting pike. Their size and colour makes them highly visible and so a good choice if the water is slightly coloured up. They are usually fitted with a large single hook rather than a treble, and can easily be provided with a weed guard to make them useable on very snaggy venues.

Spoons

In their simplest form these are just a shaped piece of metal with a hook at one end and a swivel at the other, but they catch plenty of fish. They wobble on the retrieve to represent an injured fish, reflecting flashes of sunlight as they move, making them superb for clear water venues on bright days. Top spoons include the Kuusamo Professor.

Sinking diver.

Spinner.

33

TECHNIQUES

SETTING UP

Above: Plumb up the water you are intending to fish and mark the depth on your rod. Right: When you have set up all of your tackle correctly, everything you need should be readily accessible.

EVERYBODY HAS their own way of setting up their fishing tackle and, of course, the approach you may take depends on the type of fishing you are going to do. I am going to assume that you are setting up for a day's float fishing at one peg using groundbait, and take you through my own setting-up sequence. It might not suit you completely, but you should pick up a few tips which will not only make you day's fishing more enjoyable, but will also improve your catches.

Plumbing the Depths

The very first thing I do when I arrive at a peg that I have not fished before is to set up a pole or rod and 'plumb up' the depth of the water that I intend to fish (see page 43). This might take me 10 minutes, but by the end of it I will not only have a clear idea of the depth of the swim and any underwater ledges, but also a feel for the wind direction and strength, and any tow.

I do not just plumb up out in front of me, but also to the left and right of the swim. You would be surprised how many times I have come across quite significant differences in depth by doing this. Quite often you can find a fish-holding weedbed or drop-off to one side and, in such a case, I will fish this area rather than straight out in front. By the way, if you are going to 'ball in' groundbait, it is vital to find a flat area underwater for the groundbait to settle on.

Only after I have fully plumbed up the water can I make an informed decision regarding the position from which I am going to fish, how far out I wish to cast my bait, what pattern and size of float to use etc.

Having chosen a suitable fishing spot, I mark the depth of the water at that location against the rod or pole using Tippex, measuring from the rod tip towards the handle. Then I can get on with setting up my fishing station for the session.

The Fishing Station

Now I put the keepnet into the water. There is a good reason for this, although I may not catch any fish for some time. Plumbing up and putting in the keepnet disturbs the water, and therefore the fish. By completing these tasks first, I am giving the swim plenty of time to recover while I set up my rods.

Step three is to get the seatbox positioned comfortably. I highly recommend that you invest in a box with levelling legs. Few pegs are completely flat, and without levelling legs you are not going to be comfortable when fishing, which is vital.

That done, I start arranging the accessories. You should be able to reach your landing net and keepnet easily without having to get up, and you should also be able to reach your bait, catapult, shot, hooks, disgorger and other accessories without having to move.

I then mix and riddle the groundbait because it takes about half an hour to absorb all the water fully. When mixed, I cover the groundbait with a towel to keep the sun off it.

Only then do I set up any other rods or pole sections I will be using. I do not need to plumb up again with each of these, as I can just align them against the Tippex mark I made on the first rod.

Setting up the Rods

When setting up rods, always remember to make sure that all of the rings are in a straight line, because if they are not, it will seriously affect your casting performance.

I now go back to the seatbox with a couple of bank sticks and the rods that I will be using.

For a waggler rod, the rod-rests should be set up so that the rod points directly out in front of you and the end

Above: It is a good idea to settle your keepnet in the water before you are ready to start fishing, to avoid disturbing the fish.

TEN STEPS TO SETTING UP

1 Set up one rod or pole and plumb up the depth of the water.
2 Mark the depth of water on the rod, using Tippex.
3 Place the keepnet in the water.
4 Set the seatbox up and level it if possible.
5 Sort out the landing net and accessories.
6 Mix up the groundbait.
7 Set up any other rods you might need.
8 Adjust the bank sticks and rod-rests.
9 Get the bait out of the carryall
10 Cast in your bait, throw in the groundbait and start fishing!

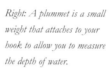

Right: A plummet is a small weight that attaches to your hook to allow you to measure the depth of water.

ring of the rod is about an inch (2.5cm) under the water when the rod is in the rod-rests. This eliminates any potential wind problems with your line.

For quivertip feeder fishing, the rests should be set up so that the rod is sideways-on to the water and the tip is about two inches (5cm) above it.

Bait and Groundbait

I am now nearly ready to start fishing. While I have been setting up, my bait has been in my carryall protected from getting too hot in the sun, and from my knocking it over as I clatter about. I have a side tray which attaches to my box on which I now put the bait.

If the groundbait has dried off a little, I will dampen it again using an atomizer filled with water. I add loosefeed to the groundbait, form it into balls and put them to the side of the box.

I then sit on the seatbox for the first time since plumbing up (hooray!). I bait the hook and cast the float out to where I want to fish, or, if I am pole-fishing, I will put the pole in pole rests at the distance I want to fish at.

I then throw the balls of groundbait in, underhand, at the float or end of the pole. I take note of where the balls have landed in relation to a static marker on the far bank, like a chimney or a tree, so that I can be certain the bait is over the feed the whole time I am fishing. Now I am ready to catch some fish.

CASTING

Cast directly over your head, rather than with the rod out to the side.

Below: Ensure that the line is loaded to the edge of the spool.

REMEMBER

If your line does not come right to the edge of the spool, you will not be able to cast properly.

CASTING ACCURATELY is far more important than many anglers believe. You might have done everything correctly so far, right to the point of plumbing your swim so the bait is just touching the bottom, giving you perfect bite registration. But unless you can accurately cast your float to the spot where you plumbed up, you are wasting your time, because the depth will probably not be the same in a different spot. You might end up with the bait a foot (30cm) from the bottom, for instance, and that could mean getting no bites.

If you are casting erratically and loosefeeding with a catapult, you are constantly moving the bait and, consequently, the fish all over your swim, instead of concentrating the fish and the bait in one small area.

The same is true if you are feeder fishing. The whole point of putting groundbait into a feeder is to try and concentrate the bait in a small area of the swim, so unless you can cast to virtually the same spot every time, you are defeating the object of the exercise.

Over Your Head

So, how do you do it? Well luckily it is easier to cast accurately than you might think. The biggest mistake many anglers make is to cast with the rod out to the side. It is

almost impossible to cast accurately doing this, as the ultimate direction depends entirely on the point at which you let go of the line.

The correct, and easiest, way to cast accurately is with the rod directly over your head pointing vertically at the sky (see picture). By casting this way, and aiming at a static marker on the far bank, the float, feeder or lead will go straight out in the same direction every time and then you only have to concentrate on trying to get the same distance with each cast, which quickly comes with practice.

Clip It Up

There is one way of making sure that the rig always goes the same distance each time you cast. If you have got a fixed-spool reel, you will probably see a strange clip on the side of the spool. This is called a line clip, and most fixed-spool reels have one. It is designed to ensure consistent distance casting.

The way to use the line clip is to cast to the point where you want to fish, tighten up the line so there is no slack, and then wrap the mainline around the line clip while the rig is still out there. You can recover your line in the normal way, and when you cast out, line will be released until it reaches the piece that is looped around the clip – exactly the same distance every time.

Using the line clip is particularly useful if you are casting quite a way, such as when feeder fishing, when judging distance can be quite difficult. The only disadvantage in using a line clip is that if you hook a really big fish which then charges off, it is likely to snap the line as you cannot release extra line from the reel, because it is fastened to the clip. For this reason, it is not recommended to use a line clip on venues holding a lot of carp or similarly powerful fighters.

HOW TO CAST

1 Select a marker on the far bank which is not going to move, like a tree or a chimney.
2 Wind the float, feeder or lead to about three feet (90cm) from the end of the rod.
3 Open the bale arm of the reel, and trap the line with your forefinger.
4 Hold the rod vertically and then point the butt of the rod at the marker, with the tip of the rod behind your head.
5 Punch the rod and rig out towards the marker, and release the line just as the momentum carries the rig towards its destination.

Left: Pick a static far-bank marker and aim the rig at it every time you cast.

Above: The line clip on your spool will ensure that you cast the same distance each time.

Look at the Spool

There is another major mistake that beginners make which prevents them from being able to cast smoothly and that is the way they have loaded the spool of the reel with line. It is essential to load the reel so that the line comes right to the edge of the spool. This ensures that line can peel smoothly off when you cast, without creating any friction.

If you have got a reel with a deep spool and cannot afford to buy enough line to fill it, wind on some wool partially to fill the spool so that it is quite close to the edge, and then wind the line over that. If your line does not come right to the edge of the spool, you will not be able to cast properly.

Finally, look at the strength of line you are using. Unless you are specimen fishing, you should not require line stronger than 4lb (1.8kg) breaking strain, and even less if you are float fishing. The stronger the breaking strain of the line, the thicker it is and the harder it is to cast with.

STRIKING, PLAYING AND LANDING FISH

THE ORANGE float tip wobbles, sways and then slowly disappears into the depths. It is that magic moment that keeps anglers returning to the water time after time. A fusion of excitement and uncertainty. Something has grabbed the bait, but what is it? Your heart beats just that little bit faster as you grab for your rod and strike.

The temptation is to wallop into the unseen fish with an almighty overhead wrench of the rod, in the hope that you will connect with something huge. Macho though this kind of energetic strike may look, I can assure you that it is not only unnecessary, but it increases your chances tenfold of losing the fish immediately. The fact is that there is

simply no need to strike aggressively. If it is a small fish that has grabbed your bait, you are likely to pull its lip off. If you have, as you hope, tempted a monster, you could be in real trouble.

If the fish is charging away from you and you exert a massive force in the opposite direction, it is probable that the line will simply snap. In either case you will end up with nothing, except your injured pride.

Don't Strike, Lift!

I do not like the word 'strike' particularly because it conjures up something dramatic. To learn how to strike properly, all you have to do is watch experienced anglers.

Above: Playing a fish with the rod held low actually brings it up higher in the water. If a hooked fish charges off in one direction, position the rod in the opposite direction to steer it away from snags.

Right: Carefully draw a beaten fish over the landing net submerged in the water. Never make a grab for the fish with your net.

LANDING PIKE

Many experts believe it is better to 'chin' pike, as shown in the picture, rather than land them in a net. However, for the beginner this is not to be advised, as pike have extremely sharp teeth, so do not attempt to chin a pike unless you are very experienced, or do not value your fingers. Land them in a net too.

When they get a bite, whether they are float fishing or legering, the 'strike' is simply a gentle 'lift' into the fish. This gentle lift is enough to set the hook, unless you are fishing at a particularly long distance, without the risk of snapping the hooklength.

Once hooked, if the fish is large and charging off, you need to give it line straight away, either by backwinding or through a lightly-set clutch on the reel. Backwinding needs explaining. All reels have a handle, and wind in one direction to bring line in. It follows that by winding the handle in the opposite direction, you can pay line out, which you do if you think a fish is going to snap your line.

There is a lever on reels known as an anti-reverse lever. Set in one position it allows you to backwind, and in its other position it switches this facility off. Either way, the reel's clutch should be set lightly so that it releases line instead of snapping it.

Ease the Fish Back

In open water you must let any good-sized fish have its first run, rather than trying to stop it. The only time you must try and stop a fish is when it is heading for a snag, and if you are fishing this type of swim you must tackle up accordingly using strong line straight through to the hook.

After the first run of the fish, it is a case of easing it back to you while keeping a tight line to the fish at all times, so that it cannot free itself from the hook.

The way to play a fish is to gently 'pump' it back to you by easing it towards you, raising the rod tip under a tight line (without winding) until the rod is vertical or level with you, then quickly winding back to the fish so it is ahead of you, and so on. If the fish charges to the left, you should position the rod to the right and vice versa. In fact, playing a fish with the rod low will actually bring the fish up higher in the water and is a good trick if you have to get a fish over a submerged ledge.

In the Net

While the fish is quite a way out you are fairly safe, because with a lot of line out you have plenty of stretch which gives you time to react if the fish suddenly decides to charge off again.

When you have got the fish within about one-and-a-half rod lengths of the bank, you must stop winding altogether because it is now at a distance for netting. This is a critical time as there is not so much stretch in the line and you should be ready to give line, with the reel's anti-reverse lever turned off.

With most species, you can tell when the fish is ready to be netted because it will come to the top and take a gulp of air. Place the landing net into the water and draw the fish over it. Never grab for the fish with the net; that will certainly spook it, and more fish are lost by this occurrence than in any other way.

All fish which are too big to 'swing' in should be landed in a landing net, and you must ensure that it is big enough to handle your target fish.

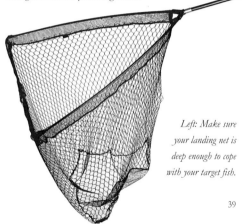

Left: Make sure your landing net is deep enough to cope with your target fish.

FLOAT FISHING – RIVERS

THERE ARE basically three ways to float fish on rivers – waggler fishing, stick float fishing and pole fishing. The latter technique is dealt with in detail on pages 44-45, so the other two methods are described here. Both involve the use of what is known as a running line, a technique in which you pay out line from the reel as the float travels downstream in the current of the water.

As was explained on pages 18-19, wagglers are attached to the line by the bottom of the float only, whereas stick floats are attached using small rings of silicone rubber tubing in 'top and bottom' fashion.

Waggler Fishing on Rivers

The waggler is a good choice for slow-flowing rivers. The float, and therefore the bait, will be carried along in the current at a slow, steady pace and will not rush past the fish so quickly that they cannot grab it.

Wagglers can be fished so that the bait is either high in the water, just touching the bottom or overdepth. Fishing overdepth slows the bait down slightly as it bumps along the river bed, and you do run the risk of snagging the bottom. For this reason you should always use a straight peacock float for this sort of fishing. This float has

Above: Use straight wagglers if you are fishing overdepth in running water.

Left: The choice of float fishing technique that you employ for rivers will depend on the speed of the flow of the water. Wagglers are best for slow-flowing rivers whereas stick floats can be easily controlled on most rivers.

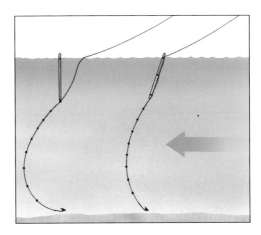

Above left: Stick floats are attached in 'top and bottom' fashion, using float rubbers.
Above: Waggler and stick float set ups.

Right: Shot your floats so that only a tiny part of the tip is showing above the surface.

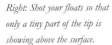

a thick tip, which has enough buoyancy to ride over slight snags without the float being dragged under the water. If you are fishing off the bottom, however, you can use a straight waggler or an insert waggler, which is more sensitive.

Wagglers should be weighted with split shot so that two-thirds of the float's ballast is bulked around the base of the float, with the rest spread out evenly down to the hooklength using small shot, such as number 8s. This produces a slow, steady fall of the bait through all layers of the water, and means that you may get bites at any depth, as the hookbait mimics the action of the loosefeed you put in.

A technique you will have to learn if you are planning to concentrate on river fishing using waggler floats is what is known as 'mending' the line. This involves carefully lifting the line from the surface of the water and putting it back behind the float every so often. This needs to be done because the upper layers of water flow faster than the lower layers. The line on the surface is carried quickly, and soon starts to pull the float through the water too fast, making the presentation of the bait appear unnatural. By mending the line, you restore good presentation of the bait.

Stick Float Fishing

Stick float fishing is a superbly enjoyable technique, which you can use on slow-, medium- or fast-flowing rivers. Because the float is attached 'top and bottom' style, you have more control over the float than when waggler fishing. This means you can alter the action of the hook

bait, and actually tease fish into taking the bait. You can run the float through the swim at the pace of the river, slow it down, hold it back hard, or vary the presentation until you find the right method for the day. If you attempted to hold a waggler back like this, it would just go under. The disadvantage of this method of float control is that it can only be practised at a short distance out from the bank, whereas a waggler can be fished at long range.

The shotting pattern should be arranged in an evenly-spaced 'shirt button' fashion for all but the strongest-flowing rivers, in which case you are better bulking most of the shot about three feet (90cm) from the hook with only two number 8 droppers below.

Casting a stick float rig is more prone to tangles than when waggler fishing. It is best done underarm, checking the line by carefully dabbing a finger on the reel's spool during the cast, so that the rig straightens out as it touches the water and does not land in a tangled heap. Stick float fishing is an art form which can take a lifetime to perfect. But it is certainly one of the most enjoyable of all fishing methods, as you are active all the time, casting, manoeuvring the rod, altering the pace of the float and, let's hope, striking into and landing fish.

FLOAT FISHING – STILLWATERS AND CANALS

STILLWATERS REQUIRE a more delicate float fishing approach than is employed for rivers because it is the fish, rather than the flow, that will pull the float under. That means that the fish have more time to feel any slight resistance and to drop the bait before the float dips. For that reason, it is vital to set the float up with the tip only just showing above the water, so that the slightest pressure will pull it under. A sensitive insert waggler is the appropriate float choice.

Unless there is a lot of undertow on the water you are fishing, four-fifths of the shot should be placed around the base of the float with perhaps two or three small dropper shot strung out down the line. The deeper the swim is and the more the tow, the more droppers you will need.

Normally the best approach is to plumb up the chosen swim at the start of the fishing session and fish so that the bait is either just touching or just off the bottom. However, in summer fish will often come into the higher layers of the water as you loosefeed, so you should be prepared to fish higher in the water if necessary.

Sinking the Line

When you cast a waggler, gently check the line just before the float lands, as this will send the rig neatly out in a straight line and prevent tangles. The rig will then settle neatly and naturally and the bait will fall slowly through the water to the bottom.

Stillwater fish are not expecting the bait to be moving once it is near the bottom, and if it does they probably will not take it because it looks unnatural to them. So if you are fishing in windy weather, you must sink the line below the water's surface to stop the wind dragging the float, and consequently the bait, all over the place. Luckily this is easy to achieve. All you have to do is to cast slightly further than the spot you want to fish, dip the rod tip under the water and wind the line in a couple of turns. This sinks the line under the water and the problem of a moving float is eliminated.

You can also buy special sprays in tackle shops which help the line to sink. You spray the line on your spool at the start of the session and it should then sink below the surface when you cast out.

Above: Float adaptors allow you to change floats quickly. Simply push the bottom of the float into the plastic adaptor.

Below right: Wagglers that are designed for canal fishing are tapered to allow for sensitive shotting.

PLUMBING UP

Plumbing up is a phrase used to describe the method of determining the depth of your swim. It is done when float fishing by using a weight which is heavy enough to pull the float under, called a plummet, attached to the end of the line. All you do is set up your tackle, estimating the likely depth of your swim, attach the plummet, and cast in. If the float sinks under the water, the swim is deeper than you predicted, if it floats on the surface, the swim is shallower. You simply have to adjust the depth of the float until its tip is situated just under the surface, and then you have established the correct depth of the water at that point.

Lift Bites

Not all bites when waggler fishing will pull the float under. If a fish picks the bait up and moves higher in the water, it will raise the lower shot with it and the float will actually rise slightly in the water. These are called lift bites and should be struck at in the same way as any other bites.

Some set-ups are actually designed to produce lift bites. They place the shot that cocks the float on the bottom, and when a fish picks up the bait, the float simply lifts up and lies flat on the surface. This is the time to strike!

Float Adaptors

A good idea for any sort of waggler fishing is always to use a float adaptor. They are designed to allow you to change floats quickly and easily, without having to disturb your rig. You simply lock the adaptor into place with split shot when you set up your tackle, and then push the base of the float into the adaptor.

They beauty of these devices is that if conditions change, or if you want to use a bigger waggler to allow you to cast further, you can just pull out the waggler you are using and place the new one into the adaptor, without having to break down the tackle completely. They are a brilliant idea and I always use them.

Waggler Fishing on Canals

On most canals the bigger fish move to the bank furthest away from the busy towpath so unless you have a very long and expensive pole, your only option is to waggler fish.

Because these 'far shelves', as they are called, are usually shallow, canal wagglers are usually quite short. However, canal fish are notoriously shy-biting so they have been designed with a tapered shape so that only a few small shot are required to take the float down the last couple of inches.

The real key to catching fish from canals is to try and cast your waggler as close to the far bank as possible, without snagging the bank itself.

POLE FISHING – RIVERS

MANY ANGLERS are uncertain about exactly what advantages pole fishing offers over ordinary rod-and-line fishing, and do not really understand why match anglers often choose the pole in preference to all other methods. Well the advantages, under certain conditions, are huge and can literally quadruple your catch compared with a conventional running line set-up, or may even result in you catching fish while other anglers catch none.

The differences that a pole makes are quite simply accuracy and presentation. With a pole it is extremely easy to plumb up the water, and when you have found the depth of your swim you can place the hook in the end of a section of the pole and mark the depth of the water on the pole itself using Tippex. This will give you a handy marker to ensure that you are always fishing at the correct depth. It is also useful to mark the distance from the bank at which you are fishing on the butt section of the pole.

This means that at all times you will know exactly where you are fishing compared to where your feed has been going in – slightly short, to the right, or precisely on the correct spot. You will also know exactly how far you are fishing off the bottom, or whether you are actually on it, just by looking at the Tippex marks.

This allows you to be so accurate that you can actually place a number 10 shot so that it is just touching the bottom with absolute confidence, or set up your pole so

that the end of the maggot is tripping the bottom. You can never be quite that accurate when fishing with a stick float, or waggler.

When you do plumb up, look for submerged ledges and if you find one fish at the bottom of it. Be sure to run the float through the swim a few times on your intended line before you feed anything, to check it is not weedy or snaggy. If it is, try a different distance.

Matching the Loosefeed

Rivers obviously flow, but not all layers of the water are necessarily moving at the same pace. The top layers of a river travel much faster than the water below it. This means that if the bait is being dragged along the bottom at the pace of the float, as it is when you are waggler fishing, the bait is behaving differently to all the loosefeed that is being gently carried along the bottom. With a pole you can change this. By holding the float back, or edging it through the water slowly, you are able to mimic the behaviour of the bait on the bottom. It really makes all the difference on

Above: Attach the rig to the pole's elastic by simply fastening a loop of line in the stonfo connector.

Left: Pole fishing is a most efficient method of catching small fish on rivers, allowing superb presentation of the bait to the fish.

Left: Floats for river pole fishing have a 'body up' shape which allows the angler to hold them back in the flow without them dragging under the water.

Right: A typical rig for pole fishing on rivers.

some days when fish are suspicious of anything out of the ordinary.

For the best results it is necessary to vary the presentation in terms of the speed at which you allow the float to move, the depth at which you are fishing and the shotting pattern you use, until you get the right combination for the day. The pole allows you to alter all these options more efficiently than any other method.

Selecting Tackle

Generally speaking, you should set the rig so that there is quite a lot of line between the pole tip and the float, as this allows you to run the float through plenty of the swim. If it is windy, you should use a number 8 back-shot positioned three inches (7.6cm) *above* the float to pull the line behind the float under the water.

Pole floats designed for river fishing have a 'body-up' shape, which means that the bulk of the shape is towards the bristle (the top end of the float). This shape is designed to allow the angler to hold the float back against the flow of the river without it dragging under. It 'rides' the flow.

The other big advantage of the pole is the elastic, which runs through the centre of the top 2-3 sections. It acts as a cushion and allows you to use fine, pre-stretched lines without fear of being broken off. Pole elastic is available in variety of different, numbered, breaking strains. Unless the flow is particularly fast, a number three or four elastic is suitable for most situations. The faster the flow and the deeper the water, the bigger the elastic you will need to set the hook and to play the fish with some degree of control.

If there are a lot of big fish around, like chub and barbel, the pole is the wrong method to use and the correct tackle would be a conventional rod and running line set-up.

If the fish are feeding on the bottom, a wire-stemmed, body-up float shotted up with an olivette and a couple of dropper shot is ideal (see diagram). If the fish are higher up in the water, it is better to use a cane-stemmed float with the shot strung out. For general fishing an ideal rig can be made up using 2lb (0.9kg) breaking strain line attached to a 1.5lb (0.7kg) hooklength.

When loosefeeding, remember to feed upstream of the float so that the feed arrives at the bottom where your hook bait is. Hemp and bronze maggot are two excellent pole-fishing baits to use on rivers, and you should remember that if you are feeding both, you should feed the maggot further upstream of the float than the hemp, as the hemp sinks faster. You should try to get all the loosefeed to hit the river bottom in the same area.

TOP TIPS

• Use body-up floats on rivers. They are designed to ride the flow.

• Poles have a length of elastic running through the middle of them which is locked in place using a bung. Most tackle dealers will set up the elastic for you.

• Rigs are attached using a simple loop connected to what is called a stonfo connector.

• Use a back shot on the line above the float when it is windy.

POLE FISHING – CANALS AND STILLWATERS

YOU CAN be even more accurate when pole fishing on canals and stillwaters than you can on rivers, because there is rarely much tow to contend with. In both cases the fish usually like to be very close to natural features, such as reeds and overhanging trees, and the pole allows you to push a float right into these features. To do this you need a very short length of line between the pole tip and the float, and this is called short-lining.

On canals you have to short-line at a distance, so you are able to reach the far-bank ledge where the big fish are to be found. On stillwaters you may have to fish a long pole to reach an island, but quite often you should be fishing really close in, almost under your feet, especially on commercial carp fisheries. In this case you need to have the pole set up behind you, so you can quickly push the pole together and chase a fish as it charges off after being hooked.

If you are groundbaiting, it is useful to locate a place where the balls will settle on a flat, rather than sloping, area of the bottom. If you throw balls onto a slope they will roll away and spread the bait over a larger area than intended. Carefully plumbing up is required.

Above: It is a huge thrill when you hook a big fish when you are pole fishing. This one was hooked during the filming of the 'Improve Your Coarse Fishing' video.

Right: The author Gareth Purnell and celebrity angler John Wilson proudly display a 7lb (3.18kg) carp which was beaten on a number 14 elastic and 5lb (2.27kg) line.

As with river pole fishing, you have some excellent presentation advantages over more traditional fishing methods when using a pole on canals and stillwaters. As well as the ability to fish virtually into snags, you can also move the bait about over your groundbait or loosefeed, dragging it from side to side or lifting it up and down. This is an excellent way of getting bites from finicky fish which may be watching the bait but only be prepared to grab it if they see it escaping.

As with any pole fishing, if it is windy you should use a back shot above the float, but another good tip is to fish overdepth in really windy conditions, with shot actually sitting on the bottom. This keeps the bait still, no matter how windy it may be above the water. The same technique applies to stillwater waggler fishing in windy weather.

Selecting Tackle

Pole floats for stillwater fishing have an elongated or a 'body-down' shape. They allow for more sensitive shotting than the body-up pattern used on rivers.

In choppy water a wire-stemmed float with an olivette set-up offers the best stability, but a more delicate presentation can be achieved by using carbon- and cane-stemmed floats with strung-out shotting patterns.

The choice of elastic and line strength required depends on the fish you are targeting. For small roach and gudgeon a No2 elastic with 1.5lb (0.7kg) line is right, for larger roach and skimmers a No3 or 4 elastic with 2lb (0.9kg) line, for big roach, small carp, tench etc., a No5 or 6 elastic with 2.5lb (1.1kg) line, for tench and bream a No8 elastic with 3lb (1.4kg) line, and for bigger carp a No10, 12 or even 14 elastic with 3-6lb (1.4-2.7kg) line.

For far-bank fishing on canals, a float called a dibber was invented. This is a very short float which is perfect for the shallow water of the far shelf. Dibbers carry only a few tiny shot yet have a big top which allows them to be used with big baits like corn, paste and luncheon meat without the weight of the bait pulling them under. They should be shotted so that the bottom shot is actually on the bottom and the bait about a foot (30cm) overdepth. Dibbers are usually used when targeting big fish, such as carp and tench, with biggish baits and should be attached with quite strong line of 3-5lb (1.4-2.3kg) breaking strain, biggish hooks sized between 14 and 16 and strong elastics ranging between number 8 and 12.

Right: Pole elastics are available in many different strengths and colours

IN YOUR CUPS

When using groundbait, many anglers use pole cups (pictured below) to make sure their bait enters the water exactly at the right spot. These cups simply clip on to the end of the pole, and are filled with balls of groundbait. The pole cup is then carefully fed out above the water to the desired fishing spot, and the pole is twisted so that the balls of groundbait fall into the water.

LEGERING – RIVERS

LEGERING IS a technique of fishing that results in the bait remaining stationary on the bottom of the river. The bait is anchored by a leger weight or swimfeeder and the end of the rod is used as a visual method of detecting bites. To allow you to detect what may be quite sensitive bites, fine quivertips have been developed which fit onto the end of rods that are designed specifically for legering. When a fish takes the bait and moves off with it, the quivertip either pulls around or drops back (see pages 20-21).

Quivertips are available in various strengths, measured in ounces, and different strengths are suitable for different venues. On very fast-flowing rivers you might need a 3oz tip, but on slower waters a 1oz tip would be a better choice.

Get the Balance Right

The secret of successful legering on rivers is to use *just enough* weight to hold the rig in place in the flow of the water. With such an arrangement, if a fish takes the bait, it will disturb this delicate balance, and the leger or feeder will move, registering a bite on the quivertip.

If the rig bounces off downriver when you cast it in, try progressively using slightly heavier weights until you find one that holds the bait without moving. Conversely, if your rig does not move on your initial cast, try using slightly lighter weights until you find one that only just holds.

Unless you are fishing close in, you must fish rivers with the rod tip high in the air, lifting as much line as possible off the water's surface. If you do not do this, the line will be drawn into a huge bow by the flow of the water and the rig will be constantly dragged out of position.

Some bites will pull the quivertip round, but more commonly with this 'rod in the air' method you will get what are called 'drop-back' bites when the quivertip bounces back towards you, as the carefully balanced feeder or lead is moved by a fish taking the bait. Quite often the fish will have hooked itself against the weight of the feeder or leger, so do not strike too hard.

Left: Carry a selection of different sized leger 'bombs' with you, to balance your rig in the flow of the river.

Above: Link legering is a good method of fishing close in.

Link Legering

The previous method is ideal if you are casting out into the middle of a river, but on some venues, and especially if the river is in flood, you are better off fishing really close in to the river bank. In these circumstances fishing with a link leger 'down the side' is a simple and effective method. All you need to do is to tie a paternoster link with a four-turn water knot (see page 51) and add two or three BB shot to the link.

Cast the rig out in front of you and let the flow bring the rig into the bank downstream of you. With this method you can fish with the rod low to the water as you would on a stillwater.

An alternative to the fixed paternoster link is to use a sliding link incorporating two small swivels, as shown in the picture above.

The Swimfeeder

Swimfeeders were developed to scatter groundbait or loosefeed around the hookbait on the bottom. On slow-flowing, deep stretches of river which hold bream you can use a groundbait feeder (see page 50), but on most rivers a 'block end' or 'maggot' feeder is a better choice. They are best attached using the rig shown on page 51.

Once you have baited the hook, take the lid off the feeder, fill it with maggots, put the lid back on and then cast out. When the feeder hits the bottom, the maggots start crawling out of the holes in the feeder and attract fish to your hookbait.

Feeders are available in a wide variety of sizes and weights and, as already described, with the 'rod in the air' method it is vital that you have enough weight on the feeder just to hold the bottom. To help you achieve the correct weight, you can buy what are called 'strap leads' or 'dead cows' which you can attach to the feeder as additional ballast.

Specimen Hunting

Big-fish anglers who target hard-fighting river species, such as chub and barbel, usually fish with large baits like luncheon meat or breadflake. Rather than using a swimfeeder to introduce bait to the swim, it is more common for the specimen angler to pre-bait several swims by hand or with a bait dropper, and then return to them and fish them one after another.

Rigs for this kind of fishing are usually quite straightforward. If fishing close in, the angler might tie a hook directly to the end of the line with no weight on it at all (called freelining), and let the bait sink and move around in the flow naturally.

If some casting weight is needed, a lead or 'bomb' can be attached on a running clip bead. Once the lead is cast in, the angler then tightens up the line to establish contact with the bait. For this method, the rod needs to be held at all times, as takes from big fish can be sudden and vicious, and could easily pull your rod in if it is left unattended in rod rests.

Above: A 'block end' or 'maggot' feeder is designed to allow maggots to crawl out of the holes and attract fish to your hookbait.

Right: A running clip bead is used to attach a leger lead.

LEGERING – STILLWATERS

APART FROM carp, stillwater fish are generally less aggressive feeders than river fish and require a more delicate approach. When quivertip legering on stillwaters, it is advisable to use the finest quivertip you can get (0.5oz) and even with this, you sometimes have to strike at the tiniest movements of the tip. One of the keys to detecting these shy bites early is to have a tight line to the rig at all times with no interference from wind. To achieve this you have to make sure that as much of the line as possible is under the water, so you must use a sinking mainline and fish with the rod low to the water. Maxima is a very popular choice of sinking mainline, and there are several other manufacturers who emblazon 'sinking' on the spools on which their line is sold.

Set your rod rests up so that the rod is out to one side of you and, when positioned in the rests, the last eye of the quivertip is only two inches (5cm) above the water's surface. This reduces any wind interference, but it also presents a problem in that there is nothing against which to judge the movement of the tip. To overcome this problem, many anglers use either a target board, as shown

below, or push a bank stick into the ground just beyond the end of the quivertip to help them detect any movement.

The Groundbait Feeder

Although you can use a groundbait or 'open-end' swimfeeder on rivers, it is a method more suited to stillwater fishing and, in particular, fishing for bream which just love to root about on the bottom looking for food.

Below: Snap swivels allow you to quickly change leads or feeders.

The feeder is simply filled by pushing it into the groundbait mixture in a container, and it is then cast out. As the feeder nears the bottom, the groundbait breaks out of the feeder and creates a lovely cloud around the hookbait, to which fish are attracted. Good loosebaits to add to your groundbait for this sort of fishing are casters, squatts and chopped-up worms.

The key to fishing using a swimfeeder is to cast accurately, so that all the feed you put into the swim is landing in virtually the same place, thus concentrating the fish in that area. To do this, you should use the line clip on the reel and follow the tips set out on pages 36-37.

Fixed Paternoster

My favourite rig for stillwater legering is the fixed paternoster rig. To create this, take a 12 inch (30cm) length of line and tie this about 12 inches (30cm) from the end of the line using a four-turn water knot (see diagram).

One of the loose ends should be trimmed tight to the knot, and the other trimmed so that you are left with a link of five inches (13cm). The feeder or lead is tied to the end of this link. The hooklength is then attached to the end of the mainline using another four-turn water knot.

Start with around three to four feet (0.9-1.2m) of line from feeder to hook but be prepared to alter this if necessary. If the fish are particularly shy you may have to use a hooklength of up to seven feet (2.1m). Alternatively, if you are getting chewed maggots but not registering any bites on the quivertip, you should shorten the hooklength until you start detecting them.

It is a good idea to use a snap swivel on the five-inch (13cm) link and attach your feeders to that. This allows you quickly to change feeders or leads should fishing conditions alter.

Bolt Rigs

Bolt rigging is a legering technique that was developed by specialist anglers who target big fish. The method depends on the use of a heavy lead, of at least two ounces (57g), and relies on confident takes from fish. The lead is fixed in place on the mainline (rather than allowed to slide freely) and when a fish picks up the bait and moves off, it actually hooks itself against the lead weight.

Bolt rigs are usually fished in conjunction with an electronic bite alarm set-up when fish such as carp and tench are the target. One of the advantages of bolt rigging is that it allows anglers to fish long sessions without having to watch the rod all the time, because there is no need to strike at a bite.

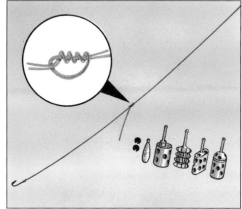

Above: Leger rig set up for stillwater fishing.

Left: The groundbait feeder is an excellent method for stillwater leger fishing. It is open ended and can be simply pushed into your container of groundbait to fill it.

DEADBAITING

DEADBAITING involves presenting all, or part of, a dead fish to try and catch predatory fish, such as pike, perch, catfish, eel or zander. The great thing about the method is that it can be really simple and may quite easily catch you a very big fish indeed. Pike grow to over 40lb (18kg) in the right conditions, and zander, a species thriving now across much of Europe, can grow to over 20lb (9kg).

Interestingly, pike in particular like sea-fish deadbaits, and among those used with great success are mackerel, herring, smelt and sardines. It is believed that the oily content of these fish is very attractive to the pike's sensitive sense of smell. However, perch, zander and eels generally will avoid taking a sea-fish deadbait, and for these species you need to use the type of coarse fish they naturally feed on, such as roach, bream, rudd and perch.

Catfish, on the other hand, are scavengers which will eat almost anything, even strips of squid or liver. For more about the most commonly used deadbaits.

Tactics

Because you are fishing for species with extremely sharp teeth, you need to use a wire trace when deadbaiting and these can be bought ready-made with treble hooks, or large single hooks, already attached.

You must match the size of your bait to your target fish and, in turn, match the size of the treble hooks on the trace to bait you are using. A decent-sized pike or catfish would have no trouble wolfing down an 8oz (227g) roach, which could be mounted on size 6 trebles. But zander, perch and eels have much smaller mouths and for these fish it is better to use a three inch (7.6cm) roach mounted on a size 8 single or size 10 treble hook.

One thing you should bear in mind when buying your bait from the fishmonger or tackle shop is the distance you are going to have to cast. Mackerel has strong skin and so is good for casting, whereas sardines will fly off the hook if you punch the cast too hard.

Deadbaits should be hooked as shown in the picture opposite, with the top treble positioned in the tail and the bottom treble in the flank. This is because predators swallow fish head first, and mounted this way, when you strike you will be pulling the hooks firmly into the upper mouth of the fish.

Using Deadbaits

There are three ways to use deadbaits – legered on the bottom, float-fished and fished 'sink and draw' style.

Sink and draw is just as it sounds; casting out a deadbait, letting it sink and them drawing it back to you

TOP TIP
On rivers, canals and drains, try deadbaiting under bridges. Bridges attract prey fish, and prey fish attract predators.

Left: Mackerel has strong skin which makes it an ideal deadbait if you intend casting some distance.

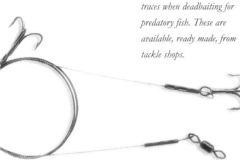

Below: You need to use wire traces when deadbaiting for predatory fish. These are available, ready made, from tackle shops.

Float-fishing the deadbait gives you a few options, because you can change the depth at which you are fishing and have an early visual warning of what pike anglers call 'a run', as a fish takes the bait. However, it is a method which I think is better reserved for livebaiting.

slowly and jerkily in a bid to mimic an injured fish. Because of this, a bait for sink and draw fishing should be whole and hooked upside down, so the dead fish is apparently 'swimming' forwards as you retrieve the line. It is the most active method of deadbaiting, and allows you to walk along the bank trying to locate the pike, rather than waiting for them to come to a static bait. However, the method relies on the fish seeing the bait from some way off and, therefore, only works well in clear water.

On venues with cloudy, coloured water, fishing a smelly, oily deadbait on the bottom is the best choice. The oils seep into the water and attract the fish to the bait. It is also a method that seems to account for the biggest fish, which are used to feeding in this way rather than chasing lively fish.

Top: Hook deadbaits with the top treble secured in the tail and the bottom hook in the flank.

Above: Baits for sink-and-draw fishing must be hooked the other way round, so that they appear to 'swim' when they are retrieved.

Left: Most pike anglers use drop-off bite alarms, set up in a similar manner to this when they are deadbaiting.

53

LURE-FISHING

Left: Use shiny silver, copper or bronze lures on sunny days when they will reflect the sunlight, and brightly-coloured fluorescent lures when the sky is overcast.

Above: Vary the speed of your retrieve; do not just cast your lure out and wind it back in a mechanical, unnatural manner. Predators respond to a jerky rhythm that imitates a wounded fish.

THERE ARE many factors to take into account when you arrive at a venue for a lure-fishing session. You need to try and think like the predator you are targeting, so as to work out where the fish is likely to be on that particular day, at what depth it might be and what sort of lure will trigger the fish into feeding.

Weather, water clarity, time of year, light conditions and natural features all play a big part in selecting the right lure. And even if you get that choice right, you have then got to work the lure in such a way that the fish will be tempted to take it.

Water Clarity

This is the most important factor of all to consider before you even start fishing. With lure fishing you are relying almost entirely on the predator's vision to get a take. It is best to restrict your lure fishing for clearwater venues. If you know there are big predators in a venue which is always coloured up, fish using a deadbait.

What Colour Lure?

This depends entirely on the prevailing light conditions. On dull days, fluorescent coloured lures, such as oranges, greens and yellows, are the best choice. On bright days, shiny silver, copper and bronze patterns will reflect the light beautifully and should be your choice. Patterns painted on the flanks of the lure can play a significant part if you are fishing in shallow, clear water, and my favourite lures are those which are adorned with a striped green and black pattern that imitates a small perch. However, if you are fishing in deep water, pattern and colour are far less important as the fish will be striking from below the lure at what appears to them as just a black silhouette.

The Best Time for Lure Fishing

On most venues predators observe set feeding times. First and last light are classic times, but there will also be times during the day when the predators feed, perhaps for only an hour. Take note of when you catch fish, and then plan subsequent sessions to coincide with these times. The time of year is also important. Generally speaking, predators will be more active in summer and that is when the best lure fishing is to be be enjoyed. However, you can also catch fish in colder weather. In winter the predatory fish are likely to have followed their prey into the deeper parts of the water where it is slightly warmer, and because the fish are not very active at this time of the year, you will need to work your lure slow and deep.

Working the Lure

A predatory fish is constantly on the look-out for any easy meal. To a pike, bass, perch, chub or zander, life is all about maximum reward for minimum effort, and the last thing they want to do is chase after fit, agile young fish all day long. To such fish an easy meal comes in the shape of an injured, dying or diseased fish which cannot easily escape

Above: Surface lures create a great deal of disturbance in the water, which often triggers predators into attacking and taking them.

capture, and that is exactly what you are trying to imitate when you retrieve your lure. Although most lures do have their own in-built action, lure fishing is certainly not just a case of casting out and reeling mechanically back in. You need to vary the speed of your lure, stop and start the retrieve, try very fast spurts followed by very slow pauses, and generally experiment with your technique until you start getting takes.

Countdown

Sinking plugs, spinners and spoons can be worked at all depths by using the countdown method. You simply cast in, and imagine the lure sinking at, say, one foot (30cm) per second. Your first few casts might be at a countdown of three seconds, working the lure three feet (90cm) deep. You can then work to a countdown of five (five feet/ 1.5m), seven (seven feet/2.1m) and so on. When you finally get a take, you may well have found the feeding depth for that day and you may then get one take after another. If you are prepared to take the risk of letting the lure sink to the bottom at each swim, you can map out any changes in depth and build up a mental picture of what the venue is like under the water.

Natural Features

Predators like to hide in natural features, such as reeds, weed beds, lilies and sunken trees, and to pounce on any unsuspecting prey fish as it passes their lair. Therefore you should try to work the lure as close as possible to any such features that you are able to cast to.

THE SPECIES

CATCHING FISH BY DESIGN

ONE OF the great joys of fishing is that you can never really guarantee what you are going to catch next. I remember attending the final of an *Angling Times* Pike Championship a few years back, in which one angler fishing a dead roach intended for pike reeled in a bemused 3lb (1.4kg) bream, and another angler fishing a spratt banked a 4lb (1.8kg) tench.

I have caught carp on deadbaits myself, just as I have caught pike on worms and perch on sweetcorn. And, of course, every so often the angler fishing a tiny bait, like a single maggot, will hook a monster carp, while the big-fish anglers all around remain fishless. But these examples are the exceptions which prove the rule. The truth is that the majority of specimen fish are caught by design, and it is only by learning more about the various species that inhabit our waters that we can maximize our chances of catching them.

Below: The author, Gareth Purnell, with a cracking catch of Irish bream. Gareth has his sights set on a double figure bream.

Below: In Britain there are thriving angling societies dedicated to catching many popular species, such as this fine catfish.

SPECIALIST FISH SOCIETIES

If you are interested in contacting one of the specialist fish societies, just ring the *Angling Times* news desk on (in the UK) 01733 266222.

As anglers progress within their sport, many will specialize in a single species; in Britain alone there are thriving societies for anglers interested in concentrating on catching tench, carp, zander, pike, perch, chub, eels, catfish and barbel.

All fish species have their own favourite feeding times, baits, flavours and different approaches are needed when fishing for them. They require different angling skills and tackle to catch them; to become a good all-round angler with the necessary skills (and tackle) to catch specimens of many different species may be a lifelong project. This is why you will hear many anglers saying that an angler never stops learning. I can honestly say that every time I go fishing, I learn something new, be it a new snippet of information about a venue, a new presentation, or just a new trick which will put more fish in my net next time.

In this section is a concise description of the 13 major coarse fish species you are likely to encounter in Britain, with a few pointers as to the best times, tactics, baits and tackle to employ to target each one. If you are fan of catching our smaller species, such as gudgeon, bleak, minnows and bullheads, tough!

It is only possible scratch the surface in these brief portraits of our wonderful fish. Whole books can, and

have, been written about each individual species, but I hope that this chapter will nevertheless interest, inform and, with luck, inspire you.

You will have your own dream fish, just as every angler has. It need not be a 40lb (18kg) carp, because there is just as much merit in catching a 3lb (1.4kg) perch, a 4lb (1.8kg) eel, a 5lb (2.27kg) chub or a 1lb (0.45kg) dace. My own dream fish is a double figure bream, and it is a dream which I fully intend to turn into reality.

There is no greater thrill in angling than successfully targeting and catching a specimen fish by design. And you just never know, your next fish just might be a record.

ROACH *(Rutilus rutilus)*

- **IDENTIFICATION:** Silver flanks, red eyes, red/orange fins, upper lip protrudes slightly over lower.
- **SPECIMEN WEIGHT:** 1lb 8oz (0.68kg).
- **LIFESPAN:** 10-15 years.
- **BRITISH RECORD:** 4lb 3oz (1.9kg), Dorset Stour, October 1990.
- **HABITAT:** Most stretches of rivers, lakes and canals.
- **TOP METHODS:** Stick float and pole.
- **BEST BAITS:** Caster, hemp, maggot.

THE ROACH, commonly known as the 'redfin' due to the orange/red fins which stand out beneath its sparkling silver flanks, is perhaps the best-loved coarse fish of all.

It may be a relative minnow when placed alongside freshwater giants such as pike and carp, yet there are many thousands of anglers who value a specimen roach above any other species. Small roach can be quite suicidal, grabbing at any bait placed in front of them. But once a roach reaches about 8oz (227g) in weight, it has been caught and returned several times and has learnt plenty. It becomes a wily old fox, which will turn its nose up at any suspicious-looking offering.

To catch big roach you must combine skill with fine tackle and watercraft, and if you do fool a fish over the 1lb (0.45kg) mark, you can be proud in the knowledge that you have succeeded where hundreds of fellow anglers have failed.

Catch a two-pounder (0.9kg) and it's time to take the camera out of the bag. And if you are ever lucky enough to slip the landing net under a magical 3lb plus (1.36kg) roach, savour every moment. This is a fish of a lifetime.

Tactics

Roach are fast-biting fish which are difficult to catch on the leger, so float fishing either with a stick float, waggler float or pole is the best approach.

When targeting river roach for instance, the pole offers the best presentation when the river is flowing slowly. A stick float is better when there is a medium to strong flow, and a waggler should be used in medium to slow-flowing conditions when you need to fish beyond the range of your pole.

TACKLING UP

Roach are finicky feeders and terminal tackle should be as fine as possible. Use size 20 and 22 fine wire hooks with maggot, and 18s and 16s with caster, making sure the whole of the hook is buried inside the shell of the caster. The force of your strike is enough to pull the point of the hook through the shell and set the hook.

A good choice for mainline for stick, waggler and pole fishing is 2lb (0.9kg) and hooklengths should be no stronger than 1.5lb (0.08mm) and finer if pole fishing, using a number 3 elastic.

Left: Stick-float fishing is a great way to catch river roach. Below: Roach are very wary fish and you may need to use light hooklengths to fool them.

SPICE IT UP

Roach love bronze maggots flavoured with a spoonful of the spice turmeric.

The correct tactics for roach do not just vary from one venue to another, they can also vary from day to day, so choosing the right method can be tricky indeed. Luckily there are some rules which you can follow to point you in the right direction.

The first thing to look at is the 'colour' of the river, stillwater or canal. If the water is crystal clear, you can rule out the use of groundbait and stick to a loosefeed approach.

Bronze maggots will get you the most bites, but casters will pick out the bigger fish. Hemp is another good loosefeed, particularly on rivers when the water is running fast.

If there is colour in the water, either washed in from a recent flood or by boat traffic or fish activity, then groundbaiting is a good idea. My favourite groundbait for roach is Van den Eynde Supercup and I will mix in some of my hookbait for the day with an initial feed of about four balls and then loosefeed over the top.

Left and below: Casters are good for picking out the bigger roach from a shoal. They should be hooked so that the shell covers the whole hook.

CARP *(Cyprinus carpio)*

- **IDENTIFICATION:** Long dorsal fin, two long barbules at corners of mouth.
- **SPECIMEN WEIGHT:** 25lb (11.3kg).
- **LIFESPAN:** Can live for over 40 years.
- **BRITISH RECORD:** 55lb 10oz (25.23kg), Wraysbury Pit, Berkshire, 1996.
- **HABITAT:** Stillwaters, canals, slow-flowing rivers.
- **TOP METHODS:** Any method.
- **BEST BAITS:** Bread, worms, boilies, corn.

Above: It is no wonder that carp anglers pursue these handsome fish.

LIKE THE Monty Python crew, you can blame the Romans. For not only were they responsible for education, aqueducts and roads, but you can also thank them for bringing carp to Western Europe some time back in the fourth century AD.

Those wild carp quickly spawned and spread throughout the rivers and lakes of Europe, but it was not until the 1400s that they were first introduced into British waters.

Now, as every angler knows, carp are among the most popular coarse fish of all. Hard-fighting, big-growing, bait-munching and line-snapping: they have captured the imagination of newcomers and seasoned specialists alike, probably because they grow larger than any other coarse fish in Britain apart from the relatively rare catfish.

Once introduced into a new venue, carp tend quickly to establish themselves as the dominant species and can easily put on 3lb (1.4kg) in weight each year.

In Europe they have been caught at weights in excess of 70lb (31.8kg), but in America, where carp are generally regarded as a nuisance to anglers in search of bass or trout, a species called buffalo carp grows to over 90lb (40.8kg).

The original, lean, majestically scaled wild carp have cross-bred many times and it is now all but impossible to find a venue that contains the true wild carp. Now it is possible to encounter commons, mirrors, leathers, linear mirrors and ghosties, to name but a few of the varieties. In addition there is the smaller crucian carp, which usually grows to no more than 7lb (3.2kg) and which hybridizes readily with the aforementioned varieties. The elongated grass carp is a more recently introduced species, which can achieve weights in excess of 30lb (13.6kg), and double that figure in warmer waters around the world.

Tactics

You could easily write a whole book about tactics for catching carp. They are wily fish which appear to learn to avoid baits on which they have been previously caught, and therefore present a wonderful challenge to the

Above: The bolt rig is designed to hook panicking carp, without the angler having to strike at bites.

thinking angler. Indeed several magazines concentrate on nothing other than carp fishing and there is even an English weekly angling newspaper dedicated to the species.

The fact is that carp will eat virtually anything when they are hungry, and the right bait on the day can be anything from a single maggot to a piece of luncheon meat the size of a Rubik's cube. Fishing is at its best during the warmer summer months when the fish are at their most active.

There is, however, one bait which has been developed specifically for the capture of carp and which is responsible for the majority of captures of really big fish – that is fish over 30lb (13.6kg) – during most of the last decade. That bait is the boilie – a highly nutritional bait which comprises a combination of milk proteins, eggs, soy flour, wheatgerm, colourings and flavourings which are moulded into a paste, and then rolled into balls and boiled to create a hard outer shell.

Boilies are naturally attractive to carp, and can be made in different sizes, with the larger ones less likely to be the target of small 'nuisance' fish. As they are basically small round balls, they are easy to disperse with a catapult which makes them ideal for pre-baiting purposes.

Bolt Rigs

Set-ups called bolt rigs were designed specifically for carp fishing, and bolt rigs and boilies go hand in hand. The bolt rig relies on the carp's tendency to panic when it feels a hook, and bolt off.

The rig's lead is locked in place rather than running, and a 2oz (57g) lead is usually enough to set the hook in the carp's mouth without the need to strike, enabling you to keep fishing without having constantly to watch the rods. Ready-made bolt rigs are generally available in tackle shops with instructions for their correct use.

Above: Many carp anglers are fond of adding weird and wonderful flavours, such as these, to their baits.

Left: Mirror carp can be identified by the large, irregular-shaped scales that appear on their flanks. Some fish are covered in these scales, while others have only a few.

BARBEL *(Barbus barbus)*

- **IDENTIFICATION:** Streamlined shape, brown flanks, rounded snout, four large barbules protruding from upper lip.
- **SPECIMEN WEIGHT:** 10lb (4.54kg).
- **LIFESPAN:** 10-15 years.
- **BRITISH RECORD:** 16lb 3oz (7.37kg), River Severn, 1997.
- **HABITAT:** Swift, well-oxygenated rivers with hard bottoms.
- **TOP METHODS:** Legering.
- **BEST BAITS:** Meat baits, maggots, hemp.

BARBEL ARE perhaps the most revered of all river coarse fish, and for many anglers the pursuit of this princely species becomes an obsession. It is little wonder, for there is no doubt that the barbel is the hardest-fighting coarse fish in the river.

When hooked, a barbel uses pure muscle power in the swift current to create an awe-inspiring, charging fight which will leave you breathless or fishless, depending on whether you are tackled up to cope with trying to stop a veritable steam train!

What's more, they grow big. In England – where the species is so popular that a Barbel Society has been formed for enthusiasts – barbel often grow to more than 15lb (6.8kg). But in Southern European countries such as Spain

Above: The barbel's streamlined, flat-bellied shape helps it hug the river beds of the fast-flowing rivers that it inhabits.

and Portugal, where the warm weather means the fish can grow throughout the year, specimens over 30lb (13.6kg) have been landed.

Tactics

Although some barbel are caught in deep, sluggish stretches of water, it is the clear, fast-flowing reaches which hold the greatest numbers. Here barbel fishing can be pursued in its purest form; stalking the river bank looking for tell-tale signs of fish moving in and out of the sweeping bottom weed.

The best tactic on these stretches is to travel light so you are able to move between swims easily and often. Start your session by walking along a stretch looking for likely barbel swims; perhaps a clear patch of gravel upstream of an area of thick streamer weed. On this clear patch you should pre-bait with particle baits such as corn and hemp, then move on.

THE DARK SIDE

Barbel will feed with the greatest confidence when it is dark, so your best bet is to make a note of the location of likely-looking swims and fish these as darkness falls.

Only when you have baited several areas should you return to your baited swims, choosing to fish only those where you can see barbel which have moved over your bait, or where your offerings have been quickly eaten.

Baits

It often pays to carry a selection of suitable baits. Specialists will usually fish large baits like cubes of luncheon meat and bunches of sweetcorn in summer, when the fish will sometimes feed aggressively, but will move on to smaller baits like maggots and casters in the winter months.

The exception is during winter flood conditions when the river is heavily coloured. Then a large, smelly bait, like a bunch of lobworms or a large lump of cheese paste, can be deadly.

On large, wide rivers where the stalking approach is not an option, the favourite method is to fish a swimfeeder. Choose a block-end feeder with a flat base and enough weight to hold steady in the current. Open up the holes in the swimfeeder with a pair of scissors, fill with hemp and casters, and cast to the same spot about 10-20 times to lay a carpet of bait on the bottom which should draw fish into your swim and hold them there.

Then you can bait your hook, and fish with the rod tip high in the air to the hold line away from the surface current and prevent the feeder being dragged out of place.

Bites will be vicious, with the quivertip bouncing dramatically back to you or right over as the fish hooks itself against the weight of the feeder. Then the battle of your life begins.

Above: A flat-bottomed feeder, with its holes enlarged, will allow tempting particle baits to escape quickly.
Right: A selection of leads will be needed for legering.

TACKLING UP

Do not bother with high-tech pre-stretched hooklengths and fine wire hooks for barbel. They will smash your tackle with embarrassing ease. To stop a powerful fish in a strong current you will need a robust sinking mainline of at least 5lb (2.27kg) breaking strain straight through to a forged specimen hook. A powerful feeder rod will be needed too to keep the fish away from snags as they charge off, and, as barbel prefer a static bait, you will also need a selection of leads, flat-sided feeders and 'strap leads' which allow you to add extra weight to your feeder to help it hold in a strong current.

Above: A cube of luncheon meat is a tried and tested bait that will often catch barbel.
Left: A specimen barbel. Fish of this size will employ their muscle power to put up a fight that you will not forget.

PIKE *(Esox lucius)*

- **IDENTIFICATION:** Camouflage markings, elongated shape, flattened head, lower jaw slightly protrudes.
- **SPECIMEN WEIGHT:** 20lb (9kg).
- **LIFESPAN:** Up to 25 years.
- **BRITISH RECORD:** 46lb 13oz (21.23kg), Llandegfedd Reservoir, Wales,1992.
- **HABITAT:** Lowland rivers, canals, drains and lakes.
- **TOP METHODS:** Livebaiting, deadbaiting, spinning.
- **BEST BAITS:** Mackerel, lamprey, roach, smelt, small pike.

SLEEK, POWERFUL, awe-inspiring and unmistakable; the pike is the top-line predator in most European freshwater fisheries and has been caught to weights approaching 70lb (31.8kg) in Europe.

Pike lead solitary lives, hiding patiently and well-camouflaged in snags, weed or reeds waiting for an unsuspecting fish to come just that little bit too close. They are built for sudden surges of speed, with the dorsal and anal fins set well back near the tail, enabling the fish to propel itself from its ambush site with frightening speed.

Prey fish are taken side on, and once grabbed in the jaws the fish has virtually no chance of escape as the upper part of a pike's mouth is lined with countless tiny, backward-pointing teeth. The pike simply manoeuvres the fish around before swallowing it head first.

Pike can swallow alarmingly large fish too, as their jaw is very flexible, allowing fish up to half that of the pike's weight to be swallowed whole. Indeed, there are several documented cases of pike choking to death after attempting to eat another pike of almost the same size as themselves!

Tactics

Young 'jack' pike up to about 12lb (5.4kg) in weight are fast and agile and able to take live prey fish with ease. However, bigger pike (all females) have more bulk to propel and will often turn to scavenging. They take dead, dying, or diseased fish and so fulfil a vital role in maintaining a healthy fishery.

Although lure fishing and livebaiting will account for plenty of pike, deadbaiting is probably the best method for trying to capture the larger fish.

Below: Instantly recognizable, the pike is a torpedo-shaped predator.

Left: Pike have flattened heads with large jaws, lined with countless tiny, sharp, backward-pointing teeth.

Baits

The choice of which bait to use is quite tricky and it is often a case of trying a variety of different sea- and coarse-fish deadbaits until you find the best one on your chosen venue. The ideal arrangement is to fish using two rods; one with a sea-fish deadbait and one with a coarse fish. To select the latter, talk to local pleasure anglers to find out what fish account for the majority of catches from the venue.

If the water is full of 4oz (113g) roach, that is what you should use as bait. But don't be afraid of big baits. If the main catch is 12oz (340g) bream, that is what the pike will be eating and that should be your chosen bait.

As for the sea bait, you should go for smelly, oily fish for starters. Mackerel tails are a proven pike bait as the oily flesh sends out a scent into the water which pike can detect from some distance. There is also a theory that a mackerel's markings are very like those of a small pike, which form quite a large percentage of a larger pike's diet.

Another proven pike catcher is the smelt, which is easy to cast without it flying off the hook due to its tough skin.

Recently another bait has taken the pike world by storm – lamprey section. Its success is undoubtedly due to

Above: Pike floats have to be large and buoyant to support deadbaits in the water.
Right: Ready-made wire traces with treble hooks, known as 'snap-tackles', are convenient for mounting deadbaits.

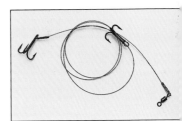

the fact that eels make up a significant percentage of a pike's diet on many venues, coupled with the fact that the bait oozes with thick blood which pike find irresistible.

Always remember that the majority of waters will have spells when the pike feed avidly, with long periods of inactivity falling in between. These feeding periods might only last for half and hour, twice a day, and it may take many hours of fishing to find out when they occur.

First and last light are often a good bet, but on hard-fished venues the 'hot' time could well be in the middle of the night, when the fish feel confident.

PERCH *(Perca fluviatilis)*

- **IDENTIFICATION:** Large erect spiny dorsal fin, dark vertical body stripes, red lower fins.
- **SPECIMEN WEIGHT:** 2lb (0.9kg).
- **LIFESPAN:** 13 years.
- **BRITISH RECORD:** 5lb 9oz (2.52kg), private lake in Kent.
- **HABITAT:** Clean reservoirs, pits, canals and slow-flowing rivers.
- **TOP METHODS:** Livebaiting, spinning.
- **BEST BAITS:** Lobworms.

THE PERCH is one of the most handsome of freshwater fish and one of the most aggressive predators too.

When young it moves in large shoals, rounding up fry and crashing through them, which results in hundreds of tiny fish leaping clear of the surface in an attempt to escape.

Because it is so aggressive, it is often the very first fish a young angler catches… and that sight of a proud predator displaying its dorsal fin to the world is often enough to hook an angler for life.

Unfortunately every few years the perch population is struck by a mystery disease which all but wipes out the entire species, but recently perch have been bouncing back with a vengeance and experts are predicting that fish weighing more than the current record are only just around the corner. Certainly in some European countries perch over 9lb (4kg) in weight have been caught.

Tactics

The real key to catching a big perch is to find a venue which contains a lot of them. This is best done by keeping an eye on the angling press for stories of big fish, and then visiting the water yourself.

There are three main ways to catch a big perch, and by big I mean any fish over 1lb (0.45kg).

Spinning is much underrated but there are (clear water) venues where this is easily the best approach as it allows you to move around and find where the perch are. The fish will usually be in the shallows close to natural features in the summer, and in deep water in the winter.

Go for a small blade spinner like the ones made by Mepps (I like the Ondex) and try and make sure there is a

TACKLING UP

Perch are not the best fighters and 5-6lb (2.3-2.7kg) main line should cope with most situations unless there are plenty of big pike present. If so, you must use a wire trace which will affect your catch rate, as perch are tackle-shy. It is better to find a venue with no pike present and fish a 4lb (1.8kg) mono hook length, although there are some very supple wires on the market now, such as Calibre.

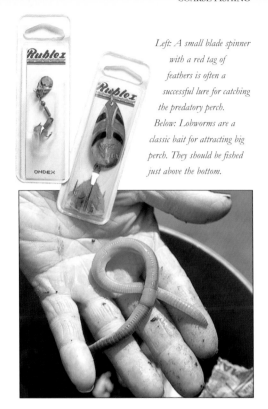

*Left: A small blade spinner with a red tag of feathers is often a successful lure for catching the predatory perch.
Below: Lobworms are a classic bait for attracting big perch. They should be fished just above the bottom.*

tag of red feathers on the back of the treble hook. This is because perch chase and peck at their prey's tail until it is unable to swim. That's when they move in and eat it. Feathers feel like the tail of a real fish and the trick is to retrieve as slowly as you dare.

The second key method is livebaiting. Choose a small livebait like a three-inch (7.6cm) roach and hook it once through the top lip with a size 6-8 wide gape hook, allowing it to swim freely under a small sliding pike float set so that the bait is about 1ft (30cm) above the bottom. Then fire maggots around the float to attract small silver fish like roach which will in turn attract perch.

The final method is good old lobworm. These are best fished on size 8 hook with a BB shot two to three inches (5-8cm) from the hook.

The worm should then be carefully injected with a small amount of air which pops it up off the bottom and allows it to wriggle enticingly. Use a clean syringe, and always air-inject the worms on a solid surface – never on the palm of your hand!

No self-respecting perch can resist this bait and freelined lobworm has accounted for some of the biggest perch ever landed.

*Above: A small roach may be used as livebait, hooked once through the top lip with a size 6-8 wide gape hook.
Left: This fine fish was caught on a small spinner. Note the perch's spiny dorsal fin and vertical body stripes.*

EARLY STARTERS

Male perch can be sexually mature at just six to twelve months even though they may be only three inches (8cm) long.

CHUB *(Leuciscus cephalus)*

- **IDENTIFICATION:** Convex dorsal and anal fins, large mouth, brassy flanks.
- **SPECIMEN WEIGHT:** 5lb (2.27kg).
- **LIFESPAN:** 10-12 years.
- **BRITISH RECORD:** 8lb 10oz (3.91kg), River Tees, 1994.
- **HABITAT:** Steady-flowing upper to middle reaches of rivers. Also found in some stillwaters.
- **TOP METHODS:** Legering big baits. Waggler and maggot.
- **BEST BAITS:** Maggots, bread, cheese paste, lobworm.

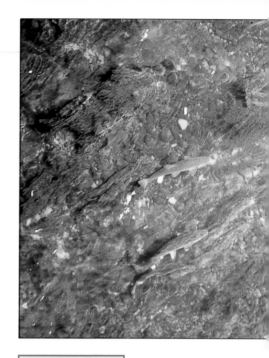

THE CHUNKY, brassy-flanked chub has been called the greediest fish in the river. Certainly it has a huge mouth capable of engulfing large lumps of bread and it is one fish that will feed all year round, even when Jack Frost is freezing the droplets of water in your rod rings.

Yet despite its reputation as a glutton which will eat almost anything, the chub is truly a wily fish and a worthy capture.

STILLWATER CHUB
Chub thrive in stillwaters and experts have predicted that the next record chub will come from a lake.

Below: A brassy-flanked chub is returned to the water. Chub can be relied on to provide sport throughout the year.

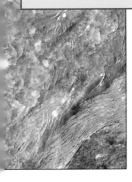

Left: Shoals of chub can often be observed picking off food in clear, fast-flowing shallows. They are extremely wary fish, however, and the slightest indication of your presence will cause these cautious fish to disappear into the surrounding weeds in a matter of seconds.

When the river is crystal clear, or at venues which are heavily match-fished, big baits are unlikely to work. Here, you should present a small bait such as single or double maggot close to, or under, the far-bank features like overhanging trees. Use a catapult to fire a healthy helping of loosefeed over your hookbait.

Maggots are the best loosefeed as they sink slowly and attract fish from far downstream. Don't use groundbait as chub hate the stuff! With the maggot method you are attempting to bring the fish into the upper layers of the water and catch them with a waggler 'on the drop' (as the hookbait sinks with the loosefeed). They can be caught as close as 12 inches (30cm) from the surface of the water.

In certain waters chub become predatory, and can be effectively targeted with spinners and spoons.

Like all members of the carp family they possess a frighteningly powerful set of bone-crushing pharyngeal teeth at the back of their throats which could easily do serious damage to your fingers should you be foolish enough to stick them inside a chub's mouth.

It is extremely rewarding to spend an afternoon silently crouched behind cover, watching a shoal of fish swaying gently with the current, picking off food. But inadvertently sneeze, or cast an accidental shadow over the water, and all the chub will disappear in seconds.

Therein lies the fascination for the angler in chub fishing. There are days when you can catch chub on a piece of cheese paste the size of a ping-pong ball and 6lb (2.72kg) line and wonder what all the fuss is about. Yet there are also times on the same venue when you need to scale down to size 22 hooks, fine lines and single maggot even to have a chance of tempting a bite.

Of course if you go too fine, you will get smashed by the chub's initial surging run. Fishing's great conundrum!

Tactics

As with many river fish, the best conditions for chub fishing are when the water is 'carrying colour'. This means that the clarity of the water has been temporarily clouded by mud washing into the river, often following heavy rainfall. Under these conditions a big, smelly bait is the best bet. Lobworms are a particular favourite, as is breadflake or paste.

It is certainly true that chub like cheese flavours and smells, and a flavour called *Scopex*, which can be sprayed onto your bait, is excellent.

Right: Always leave the tip of the hook uncovered when using breadflake as a bait. Below: Chub have huge mouths and will often readily accept surprisingly large baits. However, there are also times when only a single maggot will tempt them to bite.

TENCH *(Tinca tinca)*

Left: With its olive green hue, red eyes and slime-covered body, the tench is a handsome and distinctive fish.

1lb (0.45kg) are hardly ever caught, even by match anglers using tiny baits like bloodworm.

Tactics

Tench are essentially bottom feeders so it is not too difficult to work out where your hookbait should be. Luckily they are creatures of habit, and not only do they like particular kinds of swims, they also like to give their presence away by sending up tiny bubbles as they feed.

Classic tench venues have huge areas of lily pads which the tench love to weave in and out of. If you place a bait next to these and keep loosefeeding with your chosen hookbait, you will not go far wrong.

There is no doubt that tench feed most aggressively in the first few hours of daylight (although they are almost dormant in winter), and there is certainly a special kind of magic to watching bubbles break the surface around your float tip as the dawn mist rises off a lily-lined lake.

Float fishing is certainly a rewarding way to catch tench, and the lift method described on page 43 is a particularly deadly and enjoyable technique. But if you have to cast a long way, or you are fishing in deep water, a swimfeeder is a better bet (see page 51).

Pre-baiting

To improve your chances of a big catch of tench, you can consider pre-baiting. This is particularly important if your chosen tench venue does not boast the classic natural tench features mentioned.

By pre-baiting you can draw numbers of fish into an area you choose, which should obviously be snag-free and easy to cast to. The disadvantage is that if the lake is also full of small fish, such as roach, you will attract these as well.

- **IDENTIFICATION:** Green flanks, red eyes, paddle-like fins, two barbules on upper lip.
- **SPECIMEN WEIGHT:** 7lb (3.2kg).
- **LIFESPAN:** 20 years.
- **BRITISH RECORD:** 14lb 7oz (6.55kg), Bury Lake, Hertfordshire, 1993.
- **HABITAT:** Lakes, gravel pits, canals, slow-flowing rivers.
- **TOP METHODS:** Legering.
- **BEST BAITS:** Bread, worms, sweetcorn, maggots, casters.

Tench ARE possibly the most hardy of all coarse fish, able to live in very poorly oxygenated water and, as such, they are often the only fish to survive after a pollution incident. They are also strong fighters, and have gained a loyal following among specialist anglers, with two clubs dedicated to the species in Britain alone.

You are certainly not going to mistake the species for any other. It has a thick-set, olive green body, red eyes and tiny scales covered in a thick protective mucus which makes it beautifully smooth to touch.

Like the pike, the largest tench are all females. An 8lb (3.6kg) male is a monster, while females can grow to more than 12lb (5.4kg). However, a seven pounder (3.2kg) is still a cracker at most venues. Strangely very small tench under

DOCTOR MY RED EYES

Tench slime was thought to have magical medicinal properties in the Middle Ages and was used to treat headaches, toothache and jaundice, a practice which led to the fish being called 'the doctor fish'.

Left: The golden tench is a rare variety that is sometimes stocked in ornamental ponds.

Above: Float fishing is a pleasant and rewarding way to catch tench, like this specimen.

TACKLING UP

Tench fishing is so popular that there are rods designed specifically for pursuing the species. They usually have a test curve of about 1.5lb (0.7kg), which allows you to enjoy the fish's fight while offering more power than a standard float or leger rod. Mainline between 4lb and 6lb (1.8-2.7kg) will be strong enough for most situations, with forged hooks in size 10 and 18 required, depending on the bait used.

My favourite pre-baiting mix for tench is plain brown breadcrumb mixed with sweetcorn, casters and chopped-up worms. If I have enough time, I usually pre-bait for three consecutive days before fishing and will fish with two rods, switching between cocktails of the three baits mentioned above plus breadflake until I find the right bait for the day.

You should never use live maggots in groundbait you are going to fire in with a catapult or throw in, because they will break up the balls as they wriggle around. You can, however, use dead maggots. All you have to do is freeze some overnight to kill them before adding them to your pre-baiting mix.

Above: Bubbles rising in the water give away the presence of tench.

BREAM *(Abramis brama)*

- **IDENTIFICATION:** Bronze, slimy flanks, forked tail, downturned protruding mouth.
- **SPECIMEN WEIGHT:** 7lb (3.18kg).
- **LIFESPAN:** 15-20 years.
- **BRITISH RECORD:** 16lb 9oz (7.51kg), Buckinghamshire pit, 1991.
- **HABITAT:** Deep, slow-moving stretches of river, canal basins, deep stillwaters.
- **TOP METHODS:** Groundbait swimfeeder.
- **BEST BAITS:** Redworm, caster.

Above: The author dislays a fine brace of Irish bream. With its humped back and bronze flanks, the bream is easy to identify.

Once they reach about 1lb (0.45kg), bream tend to take on a darker appearance and as they grow older, the humped back becomes ever more prominent.

The great thing about the species as far as the angler is concerned is that the bream is a shoal fish, so if you catch one, there are almost always more in the vicinity. If you get things right, you could be in for a bumper weight of fish.

THE BREAM may not be the hardest-fighting fish in freshwater, but with its gleaming bronze flanks and humped back, a specimen bream certainly creates an impressive sight.

Small bream or 'skimmers' are silver in colour but can still be easily distinguished from other silver fish, such as roach, by their slimy sides and downturned mouths.

Tactics

Bream are bottom feeders. You only have to look at their downturned mouths to realize that they love nothing more than rooting around in the bottom silt looking for food.

Bream are also lazy creatures, unwilling to chase a bait in the same way as a nimble dace would.

For these two reasons you must present a static bait

Left: To ensure that you cast your bait accurately into a shoal of feeding bream, it is useful to use the line clip on your reel. This useful device allows you to release exactly the same length of line every time you cast.

TACKLING UP
Unless you are expecting 6lb (2.72kg) plus fish, a good choice is 4lb (1.81kg) mainline to a 3lb (1.36kg) hooklength (I like Maxima). You can use pre-stretched hooklengths with bream if you like as long as they are 0.12mm or bigger. Use the lightest quivertip you can get away with in the conditions, and strike at everything!

and the number one method is undoubtedly the groundbait swimfeeder.

With this method, each time you cast in, you can deposit more food in the swim. The key is to cast accurately, concentrating the shoal in a small area and picking off one fish after another.

As bream are not great fighters and will not tear off and break your line when hooked, you can use the line clip on the reel's spool to ensure that you cast the same distance every time. The more accurate you are, the more bream you will catch.

The fixed paternoster rig shown on page 51 is ideal for bream fishing on rivers and stillwaters.

If you think fish are shying away from the feeder, which can happen on hard-fished venues, lengthen the

hooklength to up to five feet (152cm). If the fish are coming to the feeder itself, shorten it to as little as 12 inches (30cm).

The most effective hookbait of all is a medium-sized redworm tipped with a red maggot or a caster. Cut the redworm in half and hook both of the blunt ends. The bream tend to home in on this end, resulting in more hooked fish.

The groundbait should always be at least 50 per cent plain brown breadcrumb and should always contain some chopped-up worms and some casters. Remember to riddle the groundbait before adding the bait so it breaks up nicely without forming lumps.

When you do hook a fish, steer it away from the rest of the shoal quickly so as not to spook the others. If you lose one, pray, because all too often one lost fish will scare off all the other fish with it.

Above: Always add chopped-up worms in your groundbait. Left: Small bream called 'skimmers' are silver in colour and coated in slime.

SWEET BREAM
Bream love sweet flavours, so try adding liquid molasses to the water you use to mix your groundbait.

ZANDER *(Stizostedion lucioperca)*

Above: A big zander displays its perch-like dorsal fin.

- **IDENTIFICATION:** White belly, gold flanks, green/grey back, large glassy eyes, split dorsal fin.
- **SPECIMEN WEIGHT:** 10lb (4.45kg).
- **LIFESPAN:** Up to 20 years.
- **BRITISH RECORD:** 18lb 10oz (8.39kg), River Severn, 1993.
- **HABITAT:** Lowland rivers, lakes, canals and drains.
- **TOP METHODS:** Livebaiting, deadbaiting.
- **BEST BAITS:** Roach, rudd, eel.

SOME ANGLERS mistakenly believe the zander to be a cross between a pike and perch, no doubt associating the combination of a long, slender, pike-like profile with a very perch-like dorsal fin. In truth, the zander is no relation of the pike at all, but is the biggest European member of the perch family, capable of growing to around 30lb (13.6kg) in food-rich environments.

The species is not native to English waters and was controversially introduced in 1963 when the Great Ouse River Authority released 97 small zander into the Great Ouse Relief Channel. Zander have spread quickly and can now be found in canals, stillwaters, drains and slow-flowing rivers throughout East Anglia and the Midlands, although there are none in Scotland, Wales or Ireland as far as we know.

The introduction of zander coincided with a drop-off in general coarse fishing for species like bream and roach in East Anglia, but it is highly questionable whether zander were really to blame. Certainly zander are highly efficient predators which hunt in packs when they are young, but they hunt only for food and would be sealing their own fate if they wiped out fish stocks entirely.

Tactics

Perhaps the most striking feature of your first encounter with a zander are its large, cold, glassy eyes. These are designed for hunting in low light conditions so it is hardly surprising that the best times to fish for zander are at night or when there is overhead cloud. Windy conditions which

TACKLING UP

Scaled-down pike tackle is needed. You must use a wire trace at all times with size 8-12 treble hooks, as the zander's mouth is much smaller than that of the pike. As you are always likely to hook a pike with the baits you are using, it is advisable to use 10lb (4.54kg) main line with a 1.75lb (0.8kg) test curve rod, which will give you some pleasure from the fight, yet still allow control over a big pike if you should hook one. When float fishing with livebaits, use the smallest float that you can get away with.

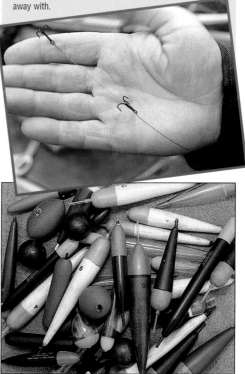

A MATTER OF TASTE

In Europe the zander, which is very similar to the American walleye, is an important sport fish and its pure white flesh makes excellent eating, although few English anglers kill them for the pot.

Above: Zander are superbly efficient predators with very sharp teeth.

Right above: Use a wire trace with small treble hooks, no bigger than size 8, to mount a small coarse-fish deadbait.

Right below: A selection of small pike floats. Use the smallest size you can when float fishing with a livebait.

create a surface ripple increase your chances of success even more.

Hot, bright, sunny days are to be avoided and, in fact, zander much prefer the darkest, most sheltered areas of the water. Only in heavily coloured fisheries or during extensive flooding, when rivers and drains run tea-coloured, will zander hunt extensively through the day.

On venues with no obvious features, like drains and canals, for instance, your best bet is to walk along the bank at dusk looking for signs of fish fry scattering as zander attack from beneath. Location is just the start of the matter though, as zander are fussy eaters which require a careful approach.

Unlike the pike, zander will not take sea-fish deadbaits and will only eat the fish it naturally consumes in the water you are fishing. In addition, they have small mouths and, as

a result, you will need to fish baits no larger than about four inches (10cm) in length. What is more, they cannot be bothered with frozen fish, much preferring recently killed deadbaits instead or, better still, livebaits caught from the fishery that day.

Finally, just to make things even more difficult, zander are very cautious if they feel any resistance, and are prone to dropping baits with hooks in them, so it pays to sit by the rods at all times and to strike immediately at any bite. However, zander present a tremendous challenge, which is why, despite the fish's relative lack of fighting prowess, a thriving zander club has sprung up in England.

RUDD *(Scardinius erythrophthalmus)*

- **IDENTIFICATION:** Golden flanks, scarlet fins, lower lip protrudes.
- **SPECIMEN WEIGHT:** 2lb (0.9kg).
- **LIFESPAN:** 10-12 years.
- **BRITISH RECORD:** 4lb 8oz (2.04kg), Norfolk Lake, 1933.
- **HABITAT:** Shallow, weedy/reedy areas of food-rich lakes, loughs and slow-flowing rivers.
- **TOP METHODS:** Float fishing.
- **BEST BAITS:** Floating casters, maggots, bread, corn.

FEW ANGLERS would argue that the true rudd is one of the most beautiful of all coarse fish, with its flanks scaled in buttery gold and its fins tipped with scarlet. However, because the species has a tendency to hybridize with roach and bream, true rudd are quite hard to find and are easily mistaken.

The best way to tell if your catch is a true rudd or not is to look at its mouth. Rudd are surface feeders and, as a result, possess a lower lip that noticably protrudes beyond the upper.

Rudd are found throughout central and southern Europe, but there is no doubt that rudd fishing has been in decline for some years, probably in deference to the more aggressive roach. In Ireland, for instance, rudd fishing used to be spectacular, but since the non-native roach was introduced around 50 years ago, the rudd population has gradually diminished.

All is not lost though, and there are still plenty of rudd left in shallow estate lakes in England and reed-fringed Southern Irish lakes and loughs.

Below: Although it hybridizes readily with roach and bream, the true rudd is one of the most beautiful of all the coarse fish, with its gold-scaled flanks and scarlet-tipped fins. Rudd are surface feeders and like to pick off insects that have fallen into the water.

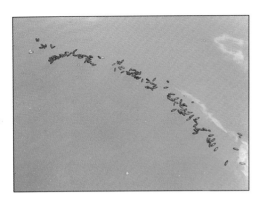

Above: It is easy to prepare floating maggots, which make an excellent bait for rudd.

Tactics

Rudd like to pick insects off the water's surface and so one of the most enjoyable and deadly of all methods for catching them is to fly-fish close to strands of reeds using small dry flies or slow-sinking nymphs.

The coarse angler without fly-fishing tackle should first try to locate the fish by feeding floating casters downwind along reed beds until fish start to show

TACKLING UP

Using an ordinary 13ft (4m) waggler rod and a reel loaded with 2lb (0.9kg) line should give you great sport. Hooklengths should be about 1.5lb (0.7kg) and the hooks should be fine wire to allow a slow, natural sink of the bait. A crystal waggler (pictured above right) and some shot completes the set-up.

Left: A line of casters floating on the water will entice rudd into feeding from the surface.

Right: Use crystal wagglers when fishing for rudd in clear water. These are less likely to scare these timid fish than large opaque floats.

RUDDY LONG RECORD

The British rudd record of 4lb 8oz (2.04kg) was set way back in 1933 and is the longest-standing of all the coarse-fish records.

themselves at the water's surface. Once you have found the fish, the best method is to fish a waggler float, fixed bottom end only, allowing you to sink the line between the rod and float to eliminate any surface drift.

Select one of the 'crystal' waggler floats, as you will be fishing in clear water and you do not want to spook a shoal of fish with a large, opaque float. Set it so that all the shot are around the float's base and only an inch (2.5cm) of the tip shows above the water, and allow two to three feet (60-90cm) of line from float to hook. Now feed a pouchful of your hookbait (maggots or casters) into the swim. When you cast in, the float should be 'checked' just before it lands so that the hook is presented in a straight line beyond the float. In this way the hookbait will sink naturally with the loosefeed and, if you have got things right, your float will sail away.

To increase your chances further, fish floating maggots on the hook. Making them float is very easy. Place a few maggots in a quarter of an inch (6mm) of water in the bottom of a bait box fitted with a lid with its centre cut out. The maggots automatically absorb air so they do not sink and drown, and within five minutes they will all be floating. The cut-out lid allows you to get at them but stops them all crawling out of the box.

Floating maggots will counterbalance the weight of the hook and either sit on the surface of the water or sink very slowly. Deadly!

DACE *(Leuciscus leuciscus)*

- **IDENTIFICATION:** Narrow, pointed head, yellow eyes, silver flanks, tail deeply forked.
- **SPECIMEN WEIGHT:** 10oz (280g).
- **LIFESPAN:** 10-12 years.
- **BRITISH RECORD:** 1lb 4oz 4drams (0.574kg), Little Ouse, 1960.
- **HABITAT:** Upper, middle and lower stretches of clean rivers, Some stillwaters.
- **TOP METHODS:** Float fishing.
- **BEST BAITS:** Maggots, casters.

ALTHOUGH THE dace is a river fish which likes to dart through the fast-flowing upper layers of water, the biggest I have ever come across were in a stillwater. To be exact, they were at Llandegfedd Reservoir, the Welsh home of the British pike record, and they averaged a whopping 10oz (280g), which by all accounts is specimen size. These fish probably came from the nearby River Usk and they illustrate the adaptability of the smallest of our 'serious' coarse fish.

Dace can be found anywhere in the river system from the fast, bubbling, upper brook stretches downwards, although they do prefer clear, clean, oxygenated water.

Above: A good-sized dace – the smallest of the 'serious' coarse fish.

Although dace are quite roach-like at first sight, you can distinguish them quite easily. Dace have yellow eyes, rather than the red eyes of the roach, and their bodies are slimmer and their heads narrow and pointed – streamlined to cope with the power of fast-flowing water.

Small chub also look a bit like dace, but chub and dace of the same length can easily be told apart by looking at the chub's mouth. It is twice as large and boasts a strong pair of rubbery lips.

Tactics

Swim selection is easy in summer, as you can usually see shoals of dace in the clear water just by wearing a pair of polarized glasses, which cut out surface glare. In these circumstances it pays to move some way upstream and fish at a distance, because if you are able to see the fish, they can see you too. On days when you cannot see any fish, choose well-oxygenated swims, such as weirpools or river confluences. Where there are no such obvious features, pick a swim where a deep hole is beginning to shallow off; these are classic swims as food will naturally build up on the bottom, attracting fish.

Below: Dace look similar to roach at first sight, but can be easily identified by their streamlined bodies, pointed heads and yellow eyes.

Below: In medium to fast-flowing water the stick float is essential to allow optimum control over the behaviour of the hook bait.

Bottom: Use maggots as loosefeed, little and often, to get the dace feeding. Then cast in your baited hook and expect quick bites as it sinks.

Dace have small mouths, and although the bigger fish will gobble up a lobworm or a big piece of breadflake without any trouble, a safer bet is to fish maggot or caster, loosefeeding little and often to keep the fish interested.

The real key to success is in the presentation of the bait, as dace are fast-biting fish and are equally quick to drop a bait once they feel any resistance. This makes them a worthy adversary despite their lack of size.

The best, and most rewarding, way of fishing for dace is to use a stick float attached both top and bottom (see page 41). Set the rig at around a foot (30cm) in excess of the depth of your swim and string out No 8s shot equally down the line in what is termed 'shirt button' fashion. This shotting pattern is vital, as it creates a steady, slow, natural-looking descent of the bait through the water.

The way to make the most of this method is to cast in so that the rig lands in a straight line beyond the float, and then to hold back hard against the flow of the river. You are trying to fool the fish into thinking that your hookbait is just another item of loosefeed, so expect the bait to be intercepted on the way down and expect bites to be fast. Be ready to strike at any movement; the float may only shudder slightly, but rest assured that a fish has taken hold of your bait.

A similar presentation can be achieved in slow-flowing or still water with a bottom-end-only waggler float, but in medium to fast-flowing water, the stick float is essential as this gives you far more control over the behaviour of the hook bait.

TACKLING UP

A 13ft (4m) waggler rod coupled with a fixed-spool or closed-face reel loaded with 2lb (0.9kg) line is ideal. The float size depends on the depth and speed of flow (a No 4 stick float would be a good starting point) and hooks should be fine wire in sizes 18-22.

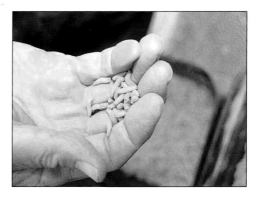

INDEX